My Modern Caribbean Kitchen

My Modern Caribbean Kitchen

70 FRESH TAKES ON ISLAND FAVORITES

JULIUS "THE CHEF" JACKSON

PAGE STREET
PUBLISHING CO.

PAGE STREET
PUBLISHING CO.

First published in 2018 by

Page Street Publishing Co.

27 Congress Street, Suite 105

Salem, MA 01970

www.pagestreetpublishing.com

Distributed by Macmillan, sales in Canada by The Canadian Manda Group.

22   21   20   19   18   1   2   3   4   5

ISBN-13: 978-1-62414-581-0

ISBN-10: 1-62414-581-7

Library of Congress Control Number: 2017962445

Cover and book design by Page Street Publishing Co.

Photography by Jennifer Blume, author photo by Donald Hebert

Author photo by Donald Hebert

Printed and bound in China

THIS BOOK IS DEDICATED TO ALL THE CARIBBEAN ISLANDS THAT HAVE BEEN DEVASTATED BY HURRICANES IRMA AND MARIA. LET US TAKE THIS AS AN OPPORTUNITY TO REBUILD AND BECOME STRONGER THAN EVER.

CONTENTS

Introduction

For many people, the Virgin Islands (VI) represent a vacation destination, known for its beaches, commerce and liveliness. But for me, it has always simply been home. My life story has been steeped and stewed in the rich history of the VI, where whispers of European architecture meet American influence and the African Diaspora. St. Thomas embodies the melting pot of the Caribbean. In a 2-mile (3.2-km) radius you can find a Jewish synagogue, a Reformed church dating back to the 1800s, stores owned and operated by East Indians, a museum reflecting the history of Denmark, a market of fourth-generation local vendors, a restaurant inspired by Italy and visitors from all over the world. It seemed natural for my cookbook to reflect this fusion of customs and cultures.

So much of the culture surrounds food. In the Virgin Islands, as in many other Caribbean islands, serving sizes tend to be large. It's not uncommon to see a plate so loaded that it looks as if the person walked through a buffet line twice. Lunch and dinner typically consist of a variety of starches, vegetables, meat, poultry and seafood, often in various combinations. Many people frequent the beach on a weekly basis and enjoy potluck-style get-togethers. I thoroughly enjoyed these days and fell in love with the kitchen at an early age. I was ten years old and very green when I prepared my first meal—fried chicken. It was late in the afternoon and my siblings and I were very hungry. I remember not having a recipe and trying to replicate what I had seen in the past done by my mom. By the time I was finished, the kitchen was a mess! It's funny to think about that moment now because little did I know it would lead to half of my life's work. The satisfaction of providing a meal that day inspired my desire to take a path toward becoming a chef. I continued fostering this desire into my early teen years when my interest also shifted in another direction.

I grew up watching my father compete at the highest level of boxing. Even as a three-time World Champion, he never tried to force me to follow in his footsteps. My brothers were interested in the sport and quickly found success. Collectively, they are part of the reason that I eventually began boxing. One day, after I got fed up with my brothers' coming home and calling me fat (I was a chubby kid), I asked my dad if I could join the gym under the condition that I could just work out and wouldn't have to compete. He agreed, and after a few months he asked me to start sparring with my brothers to help them prepare for their competitions. My eyes lit up. I said to my dad, "Wait, I get to hit them?" He said, "Absolutely!" So, I jumped right in! The first few sparring matches weren't as I'd imagined they'd be. My brothers used their experience and beat on me to the point of tears. Eventually I began to study them and learned how they were moving and timing me. I started learning the tricks of the sport and my dad took notice that I was catching up to my brothers. One day, he asked if I would consider competing and I agreed.

After my first amateur fight and victory against a kid from Barbados, I was officially in love with boxing. My passion for the sport continued to grow and I began to compete heavily in various bouts—World Games, Caribbean tournaments, Central American Games, competitive tournaments in Puerto Rico and the Golden Gloves in Florida. After each competition, my confidence grew and my skills improved. My love for the kitchen never wavered and I set my sights on being a chef and a boxer. This desire led me to enroll in culinary school shortly after graduating from high school. Balancing both boxing and the culinary arts proved challenging, but I was determined to excel at both.

Next up on my agenda was the biggest stage for an amateur fighter—the Olympics. The 2008 Olympics, held in China, were almost like a dream! Competing alongside the best athletes in the world and interacting with them in the Village was an experience of a lifetime. Although I didn't medal, I did have one of the few knockdowns during the games. It was an experience I will never forget! That was a busy year for me in both careers. I continued on parallel tracks in the kitchen and the ring. While training for the Olympics, I was still enrolled in culinary school. I completed my final semester of culinary school after returning from Beijing.

I was eager to return to the Virgin Islands and start my professional career in 2009. The transition from an amateur to a professional brought with it travel opportunities that allowed me to compete as well as experience food from many places. However, even as I continued to climb in the boxing world, the kitchen remained my sanctuary. While it can be a place of chaos (try working at a large hotel or popular restaurant where orders are coming in at a rapid pace), it generally is a peaceful environment that stimulates the five senses. The end result: a feeling of creating an experience that people will remember for some time. Perhaps an even better feeling is creating dishes from the comfort of your home for friends and family that bring you all together. That's the power of good food! This is one of my favorite experiences.

On the other hand, when I'm in the ring, it's me against my opponent. The world around me stands still and I'm toe to toe with a man trying to knock him out. The ring is a place I get to be my other self, the aggressive, strong chef! It's almost surreal to me; almost as if I'm in a movie or an out-of-body experience. I get a similar sensation when I'm in the kitchen. It's me against the critics and people who doubt me, those who want to put me in a box and doubt my ability to simultaneously perform in these dual careers I've chosen. When I'm in the kitchen, it's my opportunity to show the people I'm cooking for, and the world, just how passionate I am about food, to KO the doubts. My goal is to introduce their taste buds and palate to my culinary creations, and make sure I deliver a dining experience not soon to be forgotten.

My passion for cooking and boxing helped to create Julius "the Chef" Jackson. Inspired by the grit of the ring and the finesse of the kitchen, I am happy to serve my guests the best I have to offer! When preparing food, I believe in using fresh, locally grown ingredients whenever possible. Caribbean cuisine is one that uses many herbs and spices. This array of flavor is sure to please all who sample. In this book, I will introduce you to many of the local dishes as well as some not unique to the Caribbean but still influenced by the region. After years of cultivating my craft and putting smiles on countless faces, I have finally decided to share my passion in these pages.

This book features chapters on breakfast, lunch, dinner, snacks, drinks, soups and stews. As you read through, you will be introduced to traditional Caribbean and Virgin Islands flair—as they are cooked in my kitchen. I've grown up eating these dishes and now I have used my classical training to enhance flavors. My recipes are perfectly balanced between tradition, culture and modern techniques. If you love exploring the foods of other cultures, then this cookbook is for you. I've compiled the very best recipes of the Caribbean into one beautiful layout, ready to adorn your kitchen shelf or coffee table.

Just like the people, these dishes are diverse and influenced by various cultures. Much like a figurative melting pot, Caribbean dishes draw their inspiration from the many diverse cultures that make up the region. In addition to meals listed in this book, I have also created a chapter that I've titled "Island Fusion," in which I introduce you to recipes where I've blended Caribbean influence with my classical culinary training. Wherever possible I have provided alternative ingredients should you not be able to locate some of the recommended fare.

Thank you for inviting me into your kitchen. These are some of my favorite dishes, and I hope they will soon become some of yours.

Fully-Loaded Breakfasts

Traditional Caribbean breakfast is vastly different from the stereotypical eggs and bacon of the mainland. We use ingredients that are warm, heavy and filling because this meal is seen as fuel for the rest of the day. Breakfast is always served with tea, rather than juice or milk (check out Breakfast Bush Tea, page 153, in the drinks section). While some of the following recipes are ones you may be able to find in Caribbean restaurants, most are typically homemade, or contain ingredients you would not usually think to eat first thing in the morning. Try one of these fully loaded breakfast items and start your day with a new experience!

TRADITIONAL VI BREAKFAST

Yield: 5 servings

When you start your day off right, the rest of the day seems to go more smoothly. Here in the VI, we have a go-to breakfast meal that is not only filling and delicious, but also very healthy. Complete with fish, a well-known brain food, eggs for protein and heart-healthy vegetables, this meal has long been the breakfast of choice for Virgin Islanders.

Saltfish

1 lb (455 g) boneless salt cod

6 tbsp (84 g) unsalted butter

1 large onion, julienned

2 cloves garlic, minced

1 large red bell pepper, julienned

1 large green bell pepper, julienned

2 sprigs thyme, minced

1 (14-oz [414-ml]) can stewed tomatoes

1 tomato, roughly chopped

1 tbsp (15 g) all-purpose seasoning

1 tbsp (3 g) dried oregano

1 tsp (5 ml) hot pepper sauce

Salt and pepper

Boiled Eggs

10 large eggs

1 tbsp (18 g) salt

Okra and Spinach

2 tbsp (28 g) unsalted butter

1 large yellow onion, diced

2 cloves garlic, minced

½ lb (225 g) fresh okra, sliced

6 oz (170 g) frozen spinach

1 red bell pepper, minced

Salt and pepper

To make the saltfish: First, soak the salt cod overnight, changing the water twice. The next day, place the cod in a large pot and cover with water, then boil the fish for 10 minutes. Next, drain the fish and allow to cool for 10 minutes. Once cooled, shred the fish with a fork and be sure to remove any bones. In a large sauté pan, over medium-high heat, melt the butter and add the onion and garlic. Cook for 5 minutes, or until the onion has started to caramelize and take on a brown color. Then add the peppers and thyme and sauté for an additional 2 minutes. Add the stewed tomato and chopped tomato, all-purpose seasoning, oregano and hot pepper sauce, stir well and simmer for 5 minutes. Remove the pan from the heat and salt and pepper to taste.

To make the boiled eggs: Place the eggs in a large pot and cover with water, adding 1 tablespoon (18 g) of salt to the water. Over high heat, bring the water to a boil. Let the water boil for 2 minutes, then turn off the heat. Leave the pot on the stove and let cool for 15 minutes.

To make the spinach and okra: In a medium saucepan, heat the butter over medium-high heat. Add the onion and garlic to the pan and sauté for 3 minutes. Next, add the okra, spinach and bell pepper and stir well. Cook for 7 minutes, stirring continually. Add salt and pepper to taste.

To serve: For a traditional VI-style breakfast, place 1 scoop of the saltfish mixture, 1 scoop of the spinach and okra mixture and 2 shelled, boiled eggs on a plate. This pairs well with a side of Dum Bread (page 29) and a cup of Breakfast Bush Tea (page 153).

JOHNNYCAKES WITH CHEESE

yield: 14 servings

For a quick breakfast on the go, Virgin Islanders often stop at local food trucks, which are plentiful in the downtown Charlotte Amalie area. A johnnycake filled with cheese is a satisfying on-the-go meal that can be eaten on the way to work or school. At home, the johnnycakes can be made fresh, or leftover johnnycakes can be reheated in the toaster or toaster oven!

10 cups (1.25 kg) all-purpose flour, plus more for dusting

10 tsp (46 g) baking powder

5 tsp (30 g) salt

1 cup (200 g) sugar

2 quarts (910 ml) + ¼ cup (60 ml) vegetable oil, divided

14 slices yellow cheese (cheddar or American cheese)

In a large bowl, mix together the flour, baking powder, salt and sugar. Using a spatula, pat the mixture toward the sides of the bowl to create a well in the center. Add ¼ cup (60 ml) of vegetable oil and 5 cups (1.2 L) of water in the center and fold the wet ingredients into the dry until you have a soft, sticky dough. Let the dough sit for 5 minutes, then transfer it to a well-floured surface. Sprinkle a bit of extra flour over the dough (enough to cover the top) and knead until smooth.

Shape the dough into 3-inch (7.5-cm) balls. Sprinkle additional flour on the surface, then flatten the dough balls with a rolling pin. Then, using a knife, cut two parallel 1.5-inch (3.8-cm) slits in the center.

In a large skillet, heat 2 quarts (910 ml) of vegetable oil over medium heat until hot. Working in batches, fry the dough disks until the underside is golden brown. Flip, then cook until the next side is also golden brown.

As you remove the johnnycakes from the pan, slice each in half horizontally. Add a slice of cheese in the middle and put the halves back together, letting the heat melt the cheese. Eat it while hot!

BREAKFAST PATÉ

yield: 14 servings

This is a creation of mine born from combining some of my favorite things. Patés (pronounced pa-tays) are a main staple of Caribbean fare, in much the same way that tortillas are a backbone of Mexican cuisine. Paté dough is a blank canvas, ready to take on whatever delicious creation you can think up. Bacon and eggs is one of my favorite comfort breakfasts, and everything tastes better wrapped in fried dough, so I figured this would be a breakfast knockout. This would make a fabulous addition to your breakfast or brunch menu.

1 dozen large eggs

2 tbsp (30 ml) milk

Salt and pepper

2 tbsp (28 g) unsalted butter

½ lb (225 g) bacon, chopped

½ red bell pepper, diced

½ green bell pepper, diced

1 tomato, diced

14 oz (400 g) cheddar cheese, grated

½ batch Johnnycake dough (page 103)

All-purpose flour, for dusting

8 cups (1.9 L) vegetable oil

To begin, crack the eggs into a large bowl, then add the milk, salt and pepper, and beat with a fork until the yolks and whites are fully combined. Then, in a large skillet, heat the butter over medium heat. Add the eggs to the pan and cook, stirring often, for about 5 minutes, or until they are no longer runny. Remove the eggs from the pan and set them aside. Now, increase the heat to medium-high and add the bacon. Cook for about 7 minutes, stirring often, until the bacon is crispy. With a slotted spoon, remove the bacon from the pan and place on a paper towel–lined plate. Add the bell peppers and tomato to the bacon fat and cook for 5 minutes, or until the vegetables have softened. Transfer the vegetables to a bowl. Keep the eggs, bacon, vegetables and cheese separate so that you can add the right amount to each individual paté dough.

If the dough you are using is frozen, defrost it to room temperature. Take half of your prepared johnnycake dough and roll it out as thinly as possible, about 1⁄16 inch (2 mm), on a floured surface or parchment paper. Next, using a small bowl, cut 6-inch (15-cm) circles from the dough. In the center of each circle of dough, place a rounded heap of ¼ cup (60 g) of cooked egg, then ¼ cup (60 g) of bacon, ⅛ cup (30 g) vegetable mixture and 1 ounce (28 g) of cheese. Bring two opposite sides of the dough to meet each other around the filling to form a semicircle. Seal the rounded edges of the dough, pressing them firmly together with a fork. In a deep skillet, heat the vegetable oil to 360°F (182°C). Fry each paté until golden brown, about 7 minutes on each side. Serve hot.

SWEET AND SAVORY PUMPKIN FRITTERS

Yield: 8 servings

In the northern United States, pumpkin has come to be associated with lattes and sweater weather. But in the Caribbean, we eat local calabaza pumpkin year-round and incorporate it into soups, desserts and snacks. These pumpkin fritters taste like a delicious, savory and sweet pancake and make a great side dish or snack in between meals.

1 lb (455 g) calabaza pumpkin, or 2 cups (490 g) canned pure pumpkin puree

1 cup (125 g) all-purpose flour

1 tsp (6 g) salt

¼ cup (50 g) sugar

1 tsp (5 g) baking powder

1 large egg

1 tsp (5 ml) vanilla extract

Vegetable oil for frying

To prepare the calabaza pumpkin, first remove the skin and seeds, cut into chunks, then boil the pumpkin in water. After 15 minutes, remove the pumpkin from the water, place in a bowl and mash with a fork. Measure out 2 cups (490 g) for use in this recipe and set aside to cool. (If using canned pumpkin puree, no cooking is necessary.)

In a large bowl, whisk together the flour, salt, sugar and baking powder. Next, whisk in the egg, vanilla, mashed pumpkin and ½ cup (120 ml) of water. Mix well until the pumpkin is evenly spread throughout the batter.

These fritters can be fried two ways, according to your preference. First, to deep-fry, in a sauté pan or deep skillet, heat about 2 cups (475 ml) of oil over medium-high heat. Cook the fritters by dropping the batter by the tablespoon (15 ml) into the hot oil. Cook for about 4 minutes, until the fritters are golden brown, then flip and cook for an additional 4 minutes.

To panfry, similarly to a pancake, in a large skillet, heat 2 tablespoons (30 ml) of oil over medium heat (the pan is hot enough to add the batter when a drop of water on the pan sizzles before evaporating). Pour 2 tablespoons (30 ml) of batter per fritter onto the skillet and cook on the first side for 3 minutes, then flip the fritter and cook for another 3 minutes. Both sides should be golden brown.

Allow these to cool 2 to 3 minutes before serving.

MY MAMA'S BANANA FRITTERS

yield: 8 servings

Over the years I've noticed that people are quick to discard bananas as they start to get soft or take on dark spots. In my house, my mom never let bananas go to waste! We frequently had overly ripe bananas on hand. Smoothies are always an option when you have a few overripe bananas, but allow me to add another recipe to your repertoire—the banana fritter. A fritter is like a fluffy fried pancake, usually made with a fruit or seafood, such as conch. The beauty of the banana fritter is that it can be eaten for breakfast or as a desert with lunch or dinner. In my house, my mom is master of fritter making! I hope you enjoy this fritter recipe inspired by my mom.

¼ cup (50 g) sugar

½ tsp salt

1 tsp (5 g) baking powder

1 cup (125 g) all-purpose flour

3 cups (475 g) very ripe mashed banana

1 large egg

1 tsp (5 ml) vanilla extract

2 tbsp (30 ml) vegetable oil

In a bowl, mix together the sugar, salt, baking powder and flour. Add the mashed banana, egg and vanilla, plus ½ cup (120 ml) of water to the dry mixture and beat well until you have a thick, smooth batter. Heat the oil in a large skillet over medium-high heat. Add scoops of batter, about the size of hockey pucks (about 3 inches [7.5 cm] in diameter), to the hot oil and fry until golden brown on both sides.

Allow these to cool for 2 to 3 minutes before serving.

ISLAND-STYLE FARINA

Yield: 10 servings

In the Caribbean, we love to eat hot cereal for breakfast. The most notable thing about Caribbean-style breakfast cereals is the heavy use of warm spices. You can smell a batch of farina throughout the entire house. Islanders also love their cereals very sweet! The combination of sweet and spicy is a great way to start the day.

1 tsp (6 g) salt

2 cinnamon sticks

1 tsp (2 g) ground nutmeg

1 bay leaf

1½ cups (355 ml) whole milk

14 oz (400 g) uncooked farina cereal

1 tbsp (15 ml) vanilla extract

⅓ cup (75 g) dark brown sugar

In a large pot, combine 2 cups (475 ml) of water and the salt, cinnamon sticks, nutmeg and bay leaf. Bring to a boil over high heat, add the milk, then bring the liquid to a simmer. Next, slowly whisk in the farina and lower the heat to the lowest setting. Continue to whisk for 5 minutes, or until the mixture has thickened. Remove from the heat and whisk in the vanilla and brown sugar until fully incorporated. Remove the cinnamon sticks and bay leaf. Serve hot.

CORNMEAL PAP

yield: 6 servings

This cornmeal pap, a Jamaican dish, resembles grits but is a bit thinner in consistency. The cornmeal gives this breakfast cereal a sweet, almost nutty flavor. Unlike some other grain cereals, this doesn't need any toppings or dressings, but is full of flavor in its own right.

1 cup (140 g) finely ground cornmeal

⅓ cup (80 ml) milk, plus more if needed

1 tsp (6 g) salt

2 cinnamon sticks (optional)

1 tbsp (13 g) sugar

In a large bowl, combine the cornmeal and 2½ cups (590 ml) of water and let the cornmeal soak for 5 minutes. While it is soaking, in a medium pot, combine 2½ cups (290 ml) of water with the milk, salt and cinnamon sticks, if using, and bring to a boil over high heat. Once the water is boiling, slowly add the cornmeal mixture to the pot while whisking continuously. Lower the heat to a simmer and cook the cornmeal for an additional 15 minutes, stirring occasionally. Remove from the heat and add the sugar (and additional milk if a thinner consistency is desired). Serve hot.

DUM BREAD AND CHEESE

yield: 10 servings

The name of this bread comes from the Caribbean coal pot used for cooking that was traditionally called a dum. Modern cooks rarely use a coal pot—and this bread tastes just as delicious from the oven! The shredded coconut is optional, but highly recommended! It gives a nutty, sweet texture to this dense bread.

Nonstick cooking spray

3⅓ cups (417 g) all-purpose flour, plus more for dusting

⅓ cup (67 g) sugar

1 tsp salt

3 tbsp (41 g) baking powder

2 tbsp (30 ml) evaporated milk

5½ tbsp (83 g) salted butter

⅓ cup (67 g) shortening

¼ cup (21 g) dried shredded coconut (optional)

10 slices cheddar cheese

Preheat the oven to 350°F (180°C). Spray a baking sheet with nonstick cooking spray.

In a large mixing bowl, combine the flour, sugar, salt, baking powder, evaporated milk, butter, shortening and coconut, if using, plus ⅔ cup (160 ml) of water to form a dough. On a well-floured surface, knead the dough until smooth (this should take 10 to 15 minutes; the dough should be stiff).

Form the dough into a ball, then flatten slightly with the palm of your hand, making a more oval shape. Place the dough on the prepared baking sheet. Before placing in the oven, use a fork to prick the top surface of the dough. Bake for 35 to 40 minutes, or until light golden brown. Remove from the oven and let cool briefly, then cut into 10 wedges.

Cut each wedge in half horizontally and add a slice of cheddar cheese. Serve warm with Breakfast Bush Tea (page 153).

PICKUP SALTFISH

yield: 10 servings

Saltfish is a staple in the Virgin Islands because it has such a long shelf life. Sometimes I buy saltfish and forget I have it—leading to a pleasant surprise when I rediscover it. Saltfish can be prepared in a Creole sauce as an entrée, but pickup saltfish is a no-cook breakfast and appetizer that packs a punch. It is best when made ahead and typically eaten with crackers. Most cooks chop the ingredients by hand, but I've found that using a food processor cuts the preparation time in half. I also love the bite-size pieces, and as the peppers and onion are processed, they release all of their flavorful juices. The juices add a tremendous flavor punch that develops as the mixture is refrigerated. The peppers also give it a festive color, making it not just delicious, but a beautiful addition to your table. A common item on many holiday menus!

1 lb (455 g) boneless and skinless salt cod

½ red bell pepper

½ green bell pepper

1 yellow onion

3 tbsp (45 ml) extra-virgin olive oil

¼ cup (60 ml) white distilled vinegar

1 tbsp (15 ml) hot pepper sauce (preferably made from Scotch bonnet peppers)

Remove the cod from its packaging and rinse well. Soak the cod in water for at least 24 hours, changing the water twice. In a food processor, mince the peppers and onion. You want pieces that are small but still recognizable. Remove the cod from the water, transfer to a large bowl and shred with a fork until it is in small, flaky pieces. Remove any bones you may find. Then add the pepper mixture, olive oil, vinegar and hot pepper sauce and stir well. Refrigerate for 2 hours to give the flavors time to meld. Serve either cold or at room temperature.

Big Pot Caribbean Dishes

In the Caribbean, mealtime is family time. Whereas most of my friends in the continental United States, or as we call it simply, "the States," grew up eating meals around the television, I have many memories of sitting down at the table, eating and sharing the stories of our days with my family members. Here, food and family go hand in hand. We often serve large portions for lunches and dinners and meals are well seasoned, featuring locally sourced, whole ingredients for maximum flavor. While many of these recipes are traditional, I've rewritten some with a modern twist. Cook up one of these dishes and sit down with your loved ones!

"AS SEEN ON TV" CARIBBEAN STEWED CHICKEN

yield: 10 servings

Every region or state has its signature dish. You think Texas, you think chili. New Orleans, beignets. New York, bagels. In the Virgin Islands, stewed chicken is our signature dish. It is served at every celebration and listed on every local restaurant menu because it caters to all palates. Once you've perfected making stewed chicken, there's no doubt it will become a regular in your kitchen. My recipe truly is world famous, as it once appeared on the Cooking Channel!

3 lb (1.4 kg) chicken drumsticks and thighs

1 tbsp (6 g) poultry seasoning (preferably Goya Adobo with Pepper)

3 tbsp (45 g) sofrito, divided

3 tbsp (45 ml) olive or vegetable oil

2 large onions, julienned

2 cloves garlic, minced

2 bell peppers, julienned

3 tomatoes, coarsely chopped

3 carrots, peeled and diced

2 potatoes, diced

3 sprigs fresh thyme

½ cup (120 ml) tomato sauce

1 tbsp (15 ml) browning sauce

1 to 2 tbsp (9 to 18 g) dark brown sugar (optional)

Salt and pepper

Season the chicken with poultry seasoning and 1 tablespoon (15 g) of the sofrito. Marinate overnight in the fridge.

In a large soup pot, heat the oil over medium-high heat and brown the chicken on both sides until darker than golden but not burned. Remove from the pot and set aside.

In the same pot, combine the onions, garlic and peppers and sauté for 3 minutes over high heat while scraping down the pan. Add the browned chicken, remaining 2 tablespoons (30 g) of sofrito, and the tomatoes, carrots, potatoes, thyme, tomato sauce, browning sauce and brown sugar, if using. Add water to almost cover the chicken but not completely (about 4 cups [946 ml]). Simmer for about 45 minutes, or until the chicken is tender and falling off the bone. Salt and pepper to taste.

Serve this hot. I recommend serving with a side of Pigeon Peas and Rice (page 123) and Panfried Plantains (page 115).

BABY'S FAVORITE BAKED CHICKEN

yield: 10 servings

This recipe may not be indigenous to the Caribbean, but we do love our chicken crispy brown, very well seasoned and cooked well enough to crunch some bones—that's the sign of some really good baked chicken: When your family is around the table, even the babies are crunching away on the bones. It was a proud moment for me when my eight-month-old baby gnawed his first chicken bone. Whenever we eat this, Dominic gets to enjoy one of his favorite and yummiest teething toys!

1 tsp (2 g) freshly ground black pepper

2 tbsp (18 g) garlic powder

2 tbsp (14 g) onion powder

1 tsp (2.5 g) paprika

4 sprigs thyme, minced

1 tbsp (15 g) all-purpose seasoning

3 lb (1.4 kg) chicken parts (drumstick, thighs, wings), cleaned

2 tbsp (30 ml) olive oil

Preheat the oven to 350°F (180°C). In a small bowl, combine all the seasonings. Place the chicken in a larger bowl and coat it with the olive oil. Sprinkle the seasoning mixture evenly over the chicken and mix by hand to coat the chicken well. Place the chicken on a baking sheet, making sure to leave space in between. Bake, uncovered, for 45 minutes, or until the chicken is dark brown and crispy! Serve hot, straight from the oven. Then give your baby the bone and you will make his or her day.

ONE-POT WONDER CHICKEN AND RICE (PELAO)

yield: 8 servings

Chicken and rice is what I like to call a one-pot wonder. The rice is cooked in water along with the chicken, resulting in an extremely flavorful combination with fewer dishes to clean after. This meal featured prominently in my childhood as something frequently served at parties, as well as a dish that my mother and grandmother made often. It is also popular in Latin American countries, where it is called *arroz con pollo*. All you need are some Panfried Plantains (page 115) and a vegetable on the side and you have a complete meal.

2 lb (905 g) chicken parts (thighs with bone and drumsticks)

2 tsp (10 g) all-purpose seasoning

3 tbsp (45 ml) vegetable oil

1 large onion, chopped

2 cloves garlic, chopped

1 tbsp (9 g) diced pimiento pepper

1 whole tomato, chopped

2 cups (200 g) green olives, pitted

2 tbsp (32 g) tomato paste

2 tsp (5 g) paprika

2¼ cups (455 g) uncooked white rice

1 tbsp (13 g) sugar

Salt and pepper

If you prefer smaller pieces, cut the chicken pieces in half through the bone. Season the chicken with the all-purpose seasoning.

In a large pot, heat the oil over medium-high heat. Add the chicken and brown on each side. Mix in the onion, garlic, pimiento pepper, tomato, olives, tomato paste and paprika. Mix well until the paste is spread evenly throughout the mixture and the onion is translucent.

Next, add the rice to the pot, mix well and let cook for 5 minutes. Then add 4 cups (946 ml) of water and the sugar. Stir and then bring to a boil. Lower the heat to a gentle simmer, cover and cook for 30 minutes, or until the rice is tender and the water has evaporated. Salt and pepper to taste. Serve hot.

NO-MESS CURRY CHICKEN

Yield: 10 servings

The particular curry spice used in this recipe is a traditional Caribbean or West Indian spice, not to be confused with the East Indian curry spice. Caribbean curry powder comes in a variety of shades between yellow and green.

Other curry chicken recipes include cooking the chicken on the stovetop. However, I have found that by baking my curry chicken, the chicken comes out moister and full of flavor. This is a nice respite from standing over a stove for an hour. When I cook my curry chicken, I can put the dish in the oven, put my son to bed, come back and voilà, I've got one delicious dinner. Not to mention, one very happy wife!

Curry chicken is often served over white rice, but if you're lucky enough to know where to find traditional roti, an Indian flatbread popularly served in Trinidad, you can add a fun and equally delicious twist to your meal by stuffing your roti with the curry chicken instead.

3 lb (1.4 kg) bone-in chicken pieces (wings, thighs, drumettes)

½ cup (120 g) desired poultry seasoning

3 tbsp (35 g) curry powder

6 potatoes, diced

½ lb (225 g) carrots, cut in half lengthwise and sliced

2 large onions, julienned

1 cup (100 g) desired curry powder

Season the chicken with the poultry seasoning and curry powder, then refrigerate overnight or for at least 5 hours.

Preheat the oven to 375°F (190°C). Evenly divide the chicken, potatoes, carrots and onions between two separate baking pans. Sprinkle half of the curry powder into each pan, then mix very well. Cover the pans with aluminum foil and bake for 45 minutes. Remove from the oven and flip the chicken over. Place back in the oven and bake for another 45 minutes, leaving it uncovered this time. Turn off the oven and let the chicken sit for 15 minutes. Remove and serve hot with steamed white rice!

STEWED CONCH

yield: 10 servings

For those of us growing up on an island, the water is our playground. One of my favorite water activities is boating. It's not uncommon to come back from an afternoon of boating with a couple of snappers, some lobsters and even a few conch. A conch is a mollusk found in the Caribbean waters. It's probably most similar to eating clams, although each conch shell has much bigger pieces of meat than an individual clam. Because of the short season when you can harvest conch, it is considered a delicacy. The key to preparing conch well is the tenderizing process. Tough conch is basically inedible and definitely not enjoyable. This recipe will deliver tender and juicy conch every time.

4 lb (1.8 kg) conch, cleaned

2 tbsp (39 ml) olive oil

2 tbsp (28 g) unsalted butter

1 medium yellow onion, chopped

1 green bell pepper, chopped

1 red bell pepper, chopped

1 tsp (3 g) garlic powder

1 tsp (5 g) all-purpose seasoning

1 tsp (3 g) paprika

2 tsp (10 g) sofrito

1 Scotch bonnet pepper

1 tbsp (8 g) all-purpose flour

Salt and pepper

First, tenderize the conch by pounding with a mallet until flattened. Then place the conch in a pot of water and boil it for 1 hour. Remove from the heat and allow to cool, then remove the conch from the pot and cut into bite-size chunks. Set the conch aside. Reserve the cooking water.

In a medium pot over high heat, heat the oil and melt the butter, then sauté the onion and bell peppers for about 5 minutes. Add the garlic powder, all-purpose seasoning, paprika, sofrito and 1½ cups (355 ml) of conch cooking water and bring to a simmer. Once simmering, add the conch and whole Scotch bonnet pepper to the pan. Simmer for 7 minutes.

In a separate bowl, mix the flour with ¼ cup (60 ml) of water and stir vigorously until very well combined. Add the flour mixture to the conch mixture. Simmer for an additional 5 minutes, or until the sauce is thickened. Remove the Scotch bonnet pepper and add salt and pepper to taste. Serve hot.

NOTE: There is no close substitute for conch. It can be found in the frozen section of many stores. However, if you are unable to source conch for this recipe, you can substitute clams.

MUST-HAVE CONCH IN BUTTER SAUCE

Yield: 10 servings

If I had to compare this to a more well-known dish, I would say this is like shrimp scampi's cousin. Served in a rich, garlicky butter sauce, this conch is tender and flavorful. Conch in butter sauce is most often eaten with Fungi (page 127) and "provisions," which refers to root vegetables indigenous to the Caribbean and often includes green banana. It's important to use real butter in this recipe and not margarine to maintain the full body of the recipe.

5 lb (2.3 kg) conch

Juice of 1 lime

5 cloves garlic, thinly sliced

½ cup (120 ml) vegetable oil

1 large onion, minced

1 green bell pepper, minced

1 red bell pepper, minced

3 celery ribs, minced

3 sprigs parsley, chopped

3 tbsp (54 g) salt

1 Scotch bonnet pepper

5 tbsp (75 g) unsalted butter

Wash and clean the conch by rubbing the lime juice into the pieces. Cut the conch into 2-inch (5-cm) pieces, then place in a medium pot and cover with water. Add the garlic. Simmer over medium heat for about 2 hours to soften the conch. Remove the pot from the heat and let cool. Once the conch has cooled, drain the conch and garlic, reserving 1½ cups (355 ml) of the cooking water in a separate container to be used when making the sauce. Slice the conch into ½-inch (1.3-cm) slices. Set the conch and garlic aside.

Prepare the butter sauce by first heating the oil in a deep saucepan over medium heat. Add the onion, bell peppers, celery and parsley and sauté for 3 minutes. Add the conch and garlic to the pan and mix well to incorporate into the vegetable mixture. Then add the salt, reserved cooking water and Scotch bonnet pepper. Cook for 7 to 10 minutes. Remove the pan from the heat and gently stir in the butter. Remove the Scotch bonnet pepper and serve the conch hot!

NOTE: *There is no close substitute for conch. It can be found in the frozen section of many stores. However, if you are unable to source conch for this recipe, you can substitute boiled lobster.*

TANGY CREOLE FISH

Yield: 8 servings

When it comes to eating a plate of fish and johnnycakes, this is one of the best ways to eat it. The tangy gravy makes the natural flavor of the fish the star of the meal. Paired with a johnnycake, this meal is Caribbean comfort food at its finest. I recommend making this with snapper, but another mild white fish could easily be substituted, if necessary.

1 tbsp (15 ml) olive oil

1 large yellow onion, julienned

1 large green bell pepper, julienned

2 cloves garlic, minced

½ cup (90 g) chopped tomato

1 (8-oz [225-g]) can stewed tomatoes

⅓ cup (80 ml) white distilled vinegar

3 bay leaves

3 sprigs thyme, left whole

4 lb (1.8 kg) yellowtail snapper or mahimahi fillets

Salt and black pepper

1 tbsp (15 ml) hot pepper sauce (optional)

1 sprig parsley, chopped, for garnish

In a large, deep skillet, heat the olive oil, add the onion, bell pepper and garlic and sauté over high heat for 2 minutes, or until tender.

Then add the chopped tomato, stewed tomatoes, vinegar, bay leaves and thyme to the pan. Bring the sauce to a simmer, then add the fish fillets. Push the fish down to the bottom of the pan so the sauce covers the fish. Cover the pan and simmer for 15 minutes, or until the fish is flaking when forked. Salt and pepper to taste, add the hot sauce, if using, and stir to incorporate. Remove the bay leaves before serving.

Serve hot, with a garnish of parsley. Suggested sides: Pigeon Peas and Rice (page 123), Panfried Plantains (page 115) and Granny's Potato Stuffing (page 116).

WHELKS AND RICE

yield: 7 servings

Picking whelks is a colloquial expression used by Virgin Islanders to tease someone whose pants are too short, skimming one's ankles rather than meeting the shoes. It's quite common to hear children in the schoolyard teasing one another with the phrase. It comes from the idea that it looks as if your pants have been rolled up, so you could go wade in the shallows to look for whelks, or snails. One of the best parts of growing up in the Caribbean is year-round beach days. You might spend half the day just playing on the rocks and exploring the beach's shallow pools. And if you were lucky enough to find whelks on your adventures, you may even find them on your plate for dinner that same night!

24 whelks

2 tbsp (28 g) unsalted butter

1 large yellow onion, diced

1 large green bell pepper, diced

1 large red bell pepper, diced

2 cloves garlic, diced

6 tbsp (96 g) tomato paste

¾ cup (170 ml) tomato sauce

3 sprigs fresh thyme

2 bay leaves

Salt and pepper

1⅛ cups (225 g) uncooked white rice

1 cup (130 g) frozen corn

Place the whelks in a large, lidded pot and fill with enough water to just cover the shells. Bring the water to a boil and cook for 10 minutes. The whelks will start to come out of their shells. Drain the whelks and let them cool so that they can be comfortably handled. Shell the whelks by removing the hard front, then the intestines from the back. Roughly chop the meat and set aside.

In a large pot, heat the butter over medium-high heat. Once the butter has melted, add the onion, bell peppers, garlic and whelks and sauté for 10 minutes. Then add the tomato paste and sauce, whole thyme sprigs and bay leaves. Stir well and simmer for 20 minutes. Sample the broth and add salt and pepper to taste. Once satisfied, add 2 cups (475 ml) of water and the rice and corn to the pot and mix together. When the liquid comes to a simmer, place the cover on the pot and let cook for 10 to 15 minutes, or until the water has evaporated. Add more salt, if needed. Remove the bay leaves. Serve hot.

SLAMMIN' SALMON BALLS

yield: 6 servings

Hurricanes, unfortunately, are a part of life for those of us in the Caribbean. From a young age, we learn from our parents and elders how to prepare for and survive a hurricane. One of those skills is knowing what supplies to buy and what meals can be easily made if you are without power for days or weeks—or sometimes months!

Salmon balls are one of those meals that have sustained me following a natural disaster. The ingredients are simple, shelf stable and require only a gas stove on which to prepare them. Even the preparation method requires minimal cleanup and no fancy equipment.

3 (5-oz [140-g]) cans pink salmon
½ cup (60 g) bread crumbs
2 tsp (10 g) all-purpose seasoning
¼ cup (60 ml) extra-virgin olive oil, divided

Drain, then empty the canned salmon into a large resealable plastic freezer bag and add the bread crumbs, all-purpose seasoning and 2 tablespoons (30 ml) of the olive oil. Seal the bag and mix by hand until the ingredients are well incorporated. Heat the remaining 2 tablespoons (30 ml) of olive oil in a medium skillet over medium-high heat. Roll the salmon mixture into 1-inch (2.5-cm) balls, then flatten slightly and fry until golden brown, about 4 minutes per side.

STEWED BEEF

yield: 8 servings

This stewed beef recipe offers a Caribbean take on the all-time favorite comfort food, beef stew. In the Caribbean, cooking in a brown stew sauce is a popular preparation method applied to almost any protein. Stewed dishes are aromatic and seasoned with fresh herbs, including bay leaf, a Caribbean staple. Although in the United States beef stew is served as a soup, this dish produces a delicious gravy that is often layered over a plate of your favorite rice side dish.

1 tbsp (15 g) all-purpose seasoning

2 beef bouillon cubes

2 tbsp (20 g) minced garlic

½ cup (120 ml) white distilled vinegar

3 lb (1.4 kg) stew beef pieces

3 tbsp (45 ml) olive or vegetable oil

2 large onions, julienned

2 sweet peppers, julienned

2 celery ribs, chopped

¼ cup (60 ml) tomato sauce

2 carrots, peeled and diced

3 sprigs fresh thyme

3 bay leaves

1 tbsp (15 ml) browning sauce

1 to 2 tbsp (9 to 18 g) dark brown sugar (optional)

Salt and pepper

In a large bowl, combine the all-purpose seasoning, bouillon cubes, garlic and vinegar, and add the beef. Mix well, making sure to break apart the bouillon cubes so they blend well in the mixture. Marinate overnight or for at least 4 hours in the refrigerator.

Heat a large sauté pan over medium-high heat, then add the oil. Using a slotted spoon, scoop the beef from the bowl it marinated in and add to the sauté pan. Reserve any remaining liquid in the bowl. Cook the beef for 7 to 8 minutes, stirring often so that all sides are browned. Once the meat is browned, add the onions, sweet peppers and celery and cook for 3 minutes. Add any liquid from the marinating bowl, 2 cups (475 ml) of water and the tomato sauce, carrots, thyme, bay leaves, browning sauce and brown sugar, if using, and mix everything together until fully incorporated. Cover the pan, lower the heat to medium-low and cook for an additional 45 minutes, then salt and pepper to taste. Remove the bay leaves before serving.

SLOW-COOKED STEWED OXTAILS

yield: 10 servings

As a chef, I have many favorites, but this has to be one of my absolute favorite dishes to eat and to make. When I want comfort food, I think of stewed oxtails. I remember the first time I made them, I surprised myself by how much flavor I had created in just one dish. I'm a bone lover, which is probably why I love these so much. I love to suck out meat and marrow from every crack and crevice. This dish is loaded with flavor and has been a favorite of every crowd I have ever made it for.

5 lb (2.3 kg) oxtails, cut and cleaned

¼ cup (60 g) all-purpose seasoning

3 tbsp (45 ml) vegetable oil

3 tbsp (48 g) tomato paste

3 onions, chopped

4 cloves garlic, chopped

1 large carrot, diced

1 tsp (2 g) ground allspice

2 cups (475 ml) beef stock

2 tsp (10 ml) browning sauce

4 bay leaves

2 sprigs fresh thyme

1 Scotch bonnet pepper

1½ tsp (7 g) granulated sugar

1 tbsp (14 g) unsalted butter

Salt and pepper

Rinse the oxtails with cold water, then season with the all-purpose seasoning.

In a large, heavy-bottomed pot, heat the oil and then brown each side of the oxtails in the oil over medium heat. Once all the pieces are browned, add the tomato paste, onions, garlic, carrot and allspice to the pot. Stir well and cook for about 2 minutes, allowing the tomato paste to coat the oxtails. Add the beef stock, browning sauce, bay leaves, thyme, 1 cup (240 ml) of water, Scotch bonnet pepper and sugar to the pot and stir well. Bring to a boil, then lower the heat to a simmer. Cover the pot and let simmer for 2½ to 3 hours, or until the meat separates easily from the bones.

Once the meat is finished cooking, stir in the butter and add your desired amount of salt and black pepper. Remove the bay leaves and Scotch bonnet pepper before serving.

CURRY GOAT

yield: 8 servings

Goat is a popular alternative to beef or chicken. At times, my family would buy a goat from a local farmer or one of my uncles would catch a wild one and butcher it himself! Now, that's a true farm to table experience! Goat can sometimes be tough and benefits from a long simmer in liquid. After an overnight marinating, this recipe delivers tender goat packed full of curry flavor. Simply add rice and some Panfried Breadfruit (page 112) for a complete meal!

3 lb (1.4 kg) goat, with bones

5 tbsp (32 g) curry powder, divided

2 tsp (10 ml) white distilled vinegar

1 yellow onion, chopped, divided

2 celery ribs, chopped, divided

1 large green bell pepper, chopped

3 sprigs thyme

4 sprigs parsley

5 cloves garlic, chopped

2 tbsp (30 ml) vegetable oil

3 potatoes, cubed

2 bay leaves

1 Scotch bonnet pepper

In a large bowl, mix the goat with 3 tablespoons (19 g) of the curry powder and the vinegar. In a food processor, combine half of the onion, 1 celery rib and the bell pepper, thyme, parsley and garlic. Pulse the mixture until it is minced. Add the vegetable mixture to the goat, mix well and marinate overnight or for at least 6 hours in the refrigerator.

Next, in a large pot, heat the vegetable oil over medium-high heat. Add the remaining onion, celery rib and 2 tablespoons (13 g) of curry powder to the pot and sauté for 3 minutes. Now, add the goat to the pot and sauté for 5 minutes, or until the goat is browned. Add 4 cups (946 ml) of water and the potatoes, bay leaves and Scotch bonnet pepper and simmer, covered, for 40 minutes, or until the meat is falling off the bones. Remove the bay leaves and Scotch bonnet pepper before serving.

ROAST PORK (LECHON)

yield: 12 servings

Roast pork, also known as *lechon*, is a Puerto Rican specialty often served during the holiday season. The mark of a truly expert roast pork is extra-crispy, very flavorful skin. When you slice the roast pork to serve it, make sure you add the skin to the serving platter. The juicy, tender meat can be a main dish in its own right, or fits right in with a large holiday spread. Happy crunching!

Rub

1 tbsp (18 g) salt

1 tbsp (6 g) freshly ground black pepper

½ cup (75 g) dark brown sugar

2 tbsp (15 g) all-purpose seasoning

1 tbsp (5 g) cayenne pepper

1 tbsp (6 g) ground allspice

1 tbsp (6 g) ground cloves

2 tbsp (13 g) celery seeds

Pork

5 lb (2.3 kg) boneless pork butt or shoulder (with skin)

2 tbsp (30 ml) olive oil

To begin, make the rub by mixing all the dry seasonings together in a bowl. Next, place the pork on a cutting board and cut deep slits into the center. Then rub the pork with the olive oil, followed by the dry rub. Make sure the pork is coated well and stick your fingers into the slits to ensure the rub is under the skin as well. Cover the pork and refrigerate overnight or for 8 to 10 hours.

To cook the pork, first preheat the oven to 325°F (170°C). Place the pork in a deep roasting pan and cover it. Roast for 1½ hours. Remove the cover and drizzle the pan juices over the pork with a spoon, then roast for another hour, uncovered. Remove the pork from the oven and let it sit for 15 minutes before cutting it. The pork should peel apart easily and the skin should be very crisp.

"SATURDAY" SPECIAL SOUSE

Yield: 8 servings

Caribbean culture is famous for incorporating all the parts of animal into a dish and not letting anything go to waste. Souse is a very popular dish among older West Indians. Many restaurants feature souse only one day a week, such as Saturdays, and people make sure to show up for it. Souse is always served with a side of potato salad. It is vinegary and tender, and my favorite part about this dish is sucking the bones clean!

3 lb (1.4 kg) pork pieces (including feet and tail), unsalted

2 tbsp (30 ml) white distilled vinegar, for cleaning pork

2 celery ribs, chopped

1 yellow onion, chopped

3 bay leaves

2 sprigs parsley, chopped

2 sprigs thyme

1 Scotch bonnet pepper

Juice of 3 limes

Salt and black pepper

Clean the pork pieces with water and the vinegar, rubbing pieces thoroughly in your hands.

Place the pork in a large pot and pour in just enough water to cover the meat. Boil for 1½ hours, covered. Then drain the pork, reserving about a cup (235 ml) of broth. Return the pork to the same pot and fill with water again, barely covering the meat. Boil for 30 minutes, covered.

Next, skim the layer of froth from the top and discard, then add the celery, onion, bay leaves, parsley, thyme and whole Scotch bonnet pepper. Boil, uncovered, for 20 minutes. Drain the meat, transfer it to a large bowl and set aside.

In a separate bowl or measuring cup, combine the cup (235 ml) of broth with the lime juice and add salt and pepper to taste. Remove the bay leaves and Scotch bonnet pepper. Pour the broth mixture over the meat and serve warm with a side of potato salad.

Island Fusion

Much of the Caribbean is centered around food. In the Virgin Islands, like many other Caribbean Islands, serving sizes tend to be large—designed mostly by moms with many hungry mouths to feed while using what is easily found on island. Lunch and dinner typically consist of a variety of starches, vegetables, meat, poultry and seafood in various combinations. Similarly, recipes in Italian and French classical cuisine are also traditionally made with large families in mind. When I returned home to the Virgin Islands after completing culinary school, it seemed only natural for me to hone my skills by fusing my Caribbean background with my classical training.

One of my favorite things in the kitchen is to experiment and make meals that are out of the ordinary and not what people are expecting. I love entertaining and spending time building relationships, both new and old. Food is my offering to the people around me and it has always been a way for me to form connections. My cooking style is based on making food that feeds families and gathers people around the table. However, what you won't see much of in my recipes are the fatty cream sauces common to classical cuisine or the many fried foods often seen in Caribbean cuisine. My cooking style is heavily influenced by my athletic background, so I love using fresh ingredients and light yet super flavorful sauces. In these recipes you will see my unique blend of Caribbean, classical and athletic backgrounds! It's a crazy delicious Caribbean fusion! Enjoy!

BREAKFAST IN BED FOCACCIA SANDWICH

yield: 2 servings

I travel often and am away from home frequently. Quality time with my family is important to me and we often have to squeeze it in when we can. This recipe was born from one of those occasions. I woke up one morning and wanted to surprise my wife, who was pregnant with our son, with a special breakfast. This elevated breakfast sandwich is an elegant way to pamper your loved one, yet it comes together very quickly, giving you lots of time to surprise him or her with a special breakfast in bed!

Avocado Aioli

1 large Caribbean avocado, halved, pitted and peeled

1 clove garlic, peeled and minced

1 small white onion, minced

½ red bell pepper, minced

Juice of 1 lemon

¼ cup (60 g) olive oil–based mayonnaise (or any mayo of choice)

Salt and pepper

Sandwich

1 square loaf herbed focaccia

2 tbsp (28 g) unsalted butter, divided

2 large eggs

Salt and pepper

2 slices organic aged white cheddar cheese

1 slice prosciutto

2 slices Roma tomato

¼ cup (15 g) shredded lettuce, for garnish

Prepare the aioli: Place the avocado in a plastic mixing bowl and mash with a whisk. Add the minced veggies and lemon juice. Mix well. Then fold in the mayo until evenly distributed throughout the avocado mixture. Salt and pepper to taste.

Prepare the sandwich: Cut a 2 x 4-inch (5 x 10-cm) square from the focaccia loaf. Slice the bread horizontally, then toast it. Butter the toasted focaccia, then set aside. In a medium skillet, fry the eggs in the remaining butter, then add salt and pepper to taste. When the eggs are nearly done frying, place the cheese slices on top of the eggs so they melt slightly. Cut each slice vertically into three pieces. Take the prosciutto and cut it in half lengthwise. Remove the eggs from the pan and cut them into the shape of the focaccia squares. To create two open-faced sandwiches, place one slice of toasted focaccia on each plate, add the avocado aioli, then add the eggs, prosciutto and tomato and garnish with shredded lettuce. Serve immediately.

NOTE: *The aioli should have a nice light green color with red specks.*

CARIBBEAN QUESADILLA

yield: 10 servings

There is nothing like biting into a sweet, juicy mango and having the juice run down your face. I am lucky to have many mango trees growing in my backyard. This means mangoes have a way of working themselves onto my plate in numerous recipes. In these Caribbean quesadillas, mango provides a sweet and tangy twist. I've found this recipe pleases kids and grown-ups alike and might be a good way to sneak some healthy food into your children's meal.

2 lb (910 g) boneless, skinless chicken breast

1½ tsp (7 g) salt

1½ tsp (7 g) pepper

1½ tsp (7 g) chili powder

1 (14-oz [400-g]) can black beans, drained and rinsed

1 green bell pepper, diced

1 red bell pepper, diced

1 tbsp (15 ml) vegetable or olive oil

10 (10" [25.5-cm]) flour tortillas

2 lb (910 g) Mexican blend shredded cheese

2 large mangoes, peeled, pitted and diced into small chunks, or 2 cups (360 g) frozen mango chunks, dried

Season the chicken breast with the chili powder mixture. Grill the chicken breasts for 6 to 8 minutes per side, or until fully cooked, then set aside to cool. Once the chicken breast is cool, dice into medium chunks and set aside.

Next, in a bowl mix together the black beans and peppers. Heat the oil in a flat-bottomed sauté pan or griddle over medium heat. Place a tortilla on the pan and add cheese to the surface of the tortilla. To one-half of the tortilla, add some of the bean mixture, chicken and mango. When the cheese is melted, fold the tortilla in half. Make sure that both sides are browned. Repeat with the remaining tortillas and fillings. Cut each quesadilla into four slices and serve hot, 2 slices per serving.

LEMON PEPPER SNAPPER WITH ZESTY VEGGIE MEDLEY

yield: 5 servings

In interviews I am often asked about my favorite hobby. That's an easy answer: fishing. I love being out on the water with my family and trying to snag that big catch. Since I love to fish so much, cooking with fish comes quite naturally to me. I came up with this recipe while out in Big Bear, California, where I am the chief sparring partner for world champion boxer Gennady Golovkin. When I train with him, our workouts are especially grueling. By dinnertime, I need something that is healthy and delicious but can also be made quickly. I barely have any energy left after two workouts a day at almost 7,000 feet (2,134 meters) above sea level. I often end up cooking for a whole house full of hungry athletes. Snapper has such a crisp flavor without the overly fishy taste that some people don't care for. I like to keep my preparation of snapper simple so that its flavor comes to the forefront. Lots of fresh veggies perk up this meal, making it delicious, good for you and ready in less than 30 minutes.

5 snapper fillets (tilapia can be substituted if snapper is unavailable)

Lemon pepper seasoning

2 tbsp (30 ml) olive oil

2 tbsp (28 g) unsalted butter

2 cloves garlic, diced

2 tbsp (30 ml) freshly squeezed lemon juice, divided

1 lb (455 g) kale

½ lb (225 g) Brussels sprouts, cut in half

½ lb (225 g) mushrooms, chopped

1 red bell pepper, julienned

1 large yellow summer squash (about 4 oz [115 g]), cut in half, then sliced

1 small red onion, julienned

Zest of 1 lemon (optional)

First, rinse your fillets and dry with paper towels. Season both sides with lemon pepper seasoning to cover the fillets.

In a large sauté pan or a large grill pan over medium-high heat, panfry the fillets in the olive oil until cooked through. Set the cooked fillets aside.

Add the butter, garlic and 1 tablespoon (15 ml) of the lemon juice to the pan to deglaze it. Add the kale and sauté for 2 minutes. Cover and cook for 1 minute. Then add the Brussels sprouts to the kale mixture, cover and cook for 2 minutes. Add the mushrooms, bell pepper, squash and red onion, and sauté for 3 minutes. Add the remaining tablespoon (15 ml) of lemon juice. Sauté for 5 more minutes, then turn off the heat.

To serve, place the veggie mixture on a plate, then lay the fish fillets on top of the bed of vegetables. Garnish with lemon zest, if using.

KALLALOO PASTA

yield: 7 servings

One of the hardest parts about being a professional boxer is making it down to my fighting weight. One of my absolute favorite foods when I'm cutting weight is kallaloo, a traditional Caribbean spinach and okra soup. It is low in calories but packed with flavor and vitamins. Kallaloo often contains shellfish, pork or both. In this recipe, I combine one of my all-time favorite foods with classical preparation methods I learned in culinary school. This one-pot dish is perfect for entertaining; your guests will be wowed by the ingredient list but even more impressed by the taste.

1 ham bone

1 salt cod fillet

1 cup (240 g) unsalted butter (2 sticks), divided

2 sprigs thyme, minced, divided

1 sprig parsley, roughly chopped, divided

1 large onion, diced, divided

3 cloves garlic, diced, divided

¾ lb (340 g) crabmeat

2 lb (905 g) spinach, well rinsed and chopped

1 lb (455 g) okra, sliced

2 mahimahi fillets, chopped into 1" (2.5-cm) chunks

10 oz (280 g) whelks or mussels

10 oz (280 g) octopus (optional)

1 lb (455 g) shrimp (16/20), divided

Salt and pepper

1 lb (455 g) linguine pasta

1 tbsp (15 ml) olive oil

In a large pot, boil the ham bone and salt cod in enough water to cover for about 20 minutes. Then add about 5 cups (1.2 L) of water and let the water come to a boil. Meanwhile, heat 6 tablespoons (90 g) of the butter in a large skillet and sauté half each of the thyme, parsley, onion and garlic. When the onion is translucent, add the crabmeat and sauté for 1 minute. Remove from the heat and set aside.

Add the spinach and okra to the ham bone pot and bring back to a simmer. Add the crabmeat mixture to the pot.

In the skillet previously used for the crabmeat mixture, heat 6 tablespoons (90 g) of the butter and sauté the mahimahi, whelks, octopus, if using, and half of the shrimp for about 2 minutes, just to sear, not to thoroughly cook. Transfer this mixture to the simmering pot of kallaloo.

In the skillet that had been used for the mahimahi mixture, sauté the remaining shrimp in the remaining 4 tablespoons (60 g) of butter until fully cooked. Set the shrimp aside. Let your kallaloo simmer in the pot for 25 minutes. Salt and pepper to taste.

In a large pot, bring 7 cups (1.7L) of water to a boil. Add the pasta and boil for 10 minutes, or until al dente. Drain and place the pasta in a bowl, add the olive oil and stir, to prevent sticking. For each serving, place the pasta in a bowl first, then a large scoop of kallaloo, then garnish with 2 panfried shrimps. Serve hot.

CALABAZA AND ROAST BEEF COUSCOUS SALAD

yield: 6 servings

One of the many things I love about being a chef is taking local ingredients and making them stand out in a recipe. I am a huge fan of the local pumpkins that grow in the Caribbean. They are so creamy and sweet! Another thing that I love about cooking is surprising people with unlikely combinations. I remember the first time I served this dish at one of my Chef's Cooking Lab culinary experiences, there were definitely some skeptical faces in the crowd. However, after people actually tried this dish, it turned out to be the favorite of the night. The soft pumpkin contrasting with the crunchy chickpeas makes every bite interesting.

1 lb (455 g) calabaza pumpkin, peeled and cut into ¾" (2-cm) pieces

2 tbsp (30 ml) olive oil, divided

Freshly ground black pepper

1½ cups (355 ml) vegetable stock

1½ cups (263 g) uncooked couscous

1 (14-oz [400-g]) can chickpeas, drained and rinsed

1 cup (60 g) coarsely chopped fresh cilantro or parsley

1 lemon, halved

½ cup (15 g) rinsed, chopped spinach (optional)

½ lb (225 g) cooked roast beef strips or chunks

Salt and pepper

Preheat the oven to 350°F (180°C). Place the calabaza pumpkin in a roasting pan and drizzle with 1 tablespoon (15 ml) of the olive oil. Crack the black pepper over the top and roast for 20 minutes, or until soft.

Meanwhile, in a saucepan, combine the stock and remaining tablespoon (15 ml) of oil and bring to a boil. Remove from the heat and add the couscous. Stir, cover and set aside for 5 minutes. Use a fork to separate grains and pour into a large bowl. Add the pumpkin, chickpeas and cilantro and squeeze the lemon halves over the top. Gently mix together, add the spinach, if using, and mix to combine. Top with the beef strips. To serve, keep the pumpkin and couscous warm, but the beef can be at room temperature. Salt and pepper to taste.

CHICKEN TENDER SURPRISE WRAPS

Yield: 8 servings

My wife and I celebrated my 30th birthday with a surprise trip to Puerto Rico. I noticed that almost every dish had some form of plantain in it. Plantains are super versatile and can be a savory or sweet accompaniment to a meal, depending on how much you let them ripen. In this recipe, I combine the Caribbean love of plantains with two of my favorite things—fried chicken and pepperoni! It may seem strange, but trust me, these flavor combinations will trigger every one of your taste buds.

16 strips hot, store-bought fried chicken tenders

½ lb (230 g) pepperoni

24 pieces Panfried Plantains (page 115)

8 (12" [30.5-cm]) flour tortillas

1 lb (455 g) lettuce, shredded

1 lb (455 g) tomatoes, diced

1 lb (455 g) shredded cheddar cheese

Roughly chop the hot chicken tenders into strips and set aside. Crisp the pepperoni in a hot, dry pan over medium-high heat and set aside. Rough chop the hot plantains and set aside. To each tortilla, add these ingredients in the following order: 2 ounces (55 g) of lettuce, 2 ounces (55 g) of tomatoes, 2 chicken tender strips, 1 ounce (28 g) of pepperoni, 2 ounces (55 g) of cheese and 3 pieces of plantain. Wrap tight and serve hot.

NOTE: *Keep the ingredients hot so the cheese melts.*

ISLANDBOY STEAK RUB

yield: 1½ cups (about 220 g)

My good friend started his own spice company and I've had the pleasure of seeing it grow through the years—and being a taste tester. I developed this rub using the seafood spice, but this rub adds amazing depth of flavor to poultry, beef and pork as well. Season your steak or hamburger with a thick coating before cooking or marinate ribs in it for a few hours. You will love this!

½ cup (56 g) ground cumin

2 tbsp (32 g) salt

2 tbsp (12 g) freshly ground black pepper

½ cup (50 g) Islandboy Spices Seafood Tsunami (see note)

⅓ cup (50 g) dark brown sugar

7 cloves garlic, minced

In a bowl, mix all the ingredients together and store in an airtight container in the refrigerator. Keeps for up to 6 months.

NOTE: *Visit www.islandboyspices.com or www.facebook.islandboyspices/ if you cannot find this blend locally.*

If you cannot purchase Islandboy Spices Seafood Tsunami, you can substitute your own mixture with 4½ tablespoons (67 g) of dried onions, 2 tablespoons (30 g) of garlic powder, ½ tablespoon (7 g) of lemon powder and 1 tablespoon (12 g) of paprika.

Top-Ranked Soups

Soup is a staple throughout the islands of the Caribbean. Caribbean people have always lived off the land and relied on less expensive ingredients to create meals. Traditionally, West Indians without access to a stove used coal pots as a heating source. Coal pots are best used for boiling, which creates a perfect canvas for turning simple ingredients into delectable dishes. Affordable ingredients, such as beans, pig extremities, okra and fish are used in my modern take on these classic soup recipes!

M.B.W. FAMOUS CHICKEN PUMPKIN SOUP

Yield: 10 servings

In St. Thomas, I work for a nonprofit organization, called My Brother's Workshop, which mentors and trains at-risk youth in real-world skills. The goal is to empower and give them hope so they can become the best versions of themselves and go after their goals and dreams. One of our programs is a bakery and café of which I am manager and head chef. Here is our signature soup served in the café. We have customers who make sure they don't miss "Pumpkin Soup Wednesdays." I love that the pumpkin makes this soup just a touch sweet and super creamy. It's also nice to know that every bite is loaded with vitamins.

1 tbsp (15 ml) olive oil

1 large yellow onion, chopped

2 large carrots, peeled and chopped

2 celery ribs, chopped

1 large green bell pepper, chopped

1 large red bell pepper, chopped

2 cloves garlic, minced

3 sprigs fresh thyme, minced

2 tbsp (30 g) dry taragon

2 tbsp (30 g) all-purpose seasoning

2½ lb (1.1 kg) chicken breast, cubed

4 potatoes, cubed

2 cups (490 ml) pure pumpkin puree

3 cups (710 ml) chicken stock

1 batch Down Island Dumpling dough (page 128), cut into 2" (5-cm) pieces

Salt and pepper

In a large pot, heat oil over medium-high heat, then add the onion, carrots, celery, bell peppers and garlic, and sauté for 5 minutes. Next, add the thyme, taragon, all-purpose seasoning and chicken. Mix well to coat all the ingredients with the seasonings. Cook for 7 minutes, then add the potatoes. Mix well until incorporated, then add the pumpkin, chicken stock and 7 cups (1.7 L) of water. Bring to a boil, then lower the heat to a simmer and let cook for an additional 20 minutes. Add the dumpling dough and cook for 10 more minutes. Salt and pepper to taste.

OLD-TIME CHICKEN SOUP

yield: 10 servings

It doesn't get much better than a bowl of chicken soup. Instead of adding noodles, the soup I have perfected has dumplings, which adds a tasty twist and makes the soup even heartier. I love to make chicken soup when family is coming over because one pot can stretch to make sure everyone has eaten their fill! Easily Virgin Islanders' most popular soup!

2 tbsp (30 ml) vegetable oil

1 large onion, diced

1 large green bell pepper, diced

1 large red bell pepper, diced

1 celery rib, diced

3 cloves garlic, minced

1 Scotch bonnet pepper

3 large potatoes, cubed

2 large carrots, diced

3 cups (270 g) cubed white cabbage

4 sprigs thyme

1 tbsp (4 g) chopped fresh parsley leaves

4 bay leaves

3 lb (1.4 kg) bone-in chicken wings

8 cups (1.9 L) chicken stock

1 batch Down Island Dumpling dough (page 128), cut into 1" (2.5-cm) pieces

Salt and pepper

In a large soup pot, heat the oil and sauté the onion, bell peppers, celery, and garlic over medium-high heat for 7 minutes. Then add the Scotch bonnet pepper, potatoes, carrots, cabbage, thyme, parsley, bay leaves, chicken wings, chicken stock and 8 cups (1.9 L) of water. Bring the soup to a boil and then lower the heat to a simmer. Cover and cook for 1¼ hours, or until the chicken is falling off the bone, then add the dumplings and cook for 10 minutes longer. Remove the bay leaves and Scotch bonnet pepper. Salt and pepper to taste and serve hot!

GOAT WATER

yield: 10 servings

Whoever named this stew really didn't do it any favors. I know goat water probably doesn't sound like much, but trust me, this soup is brimming with flavor. The heart of the soup is in the broth, which cooks for over two hours, developing a deep, rich flavor profile. Pair this soup with a crusty bread and you have a hearty meal. This soup is the island of Montserrat's national dish!

5 lb (2.3 kg) goat meat, cleaned

¼ cup (60 ml) white distilled vinegar, for cleaning goat

¼ cup (60 ml) vegetable oil

2 tbsp (32 g) tomato paste

1 large yellow onion, diced

3 cloves garlic, minced

1 green bell pepper, chopped

1 red bell pepper, chopped

3 celery ribs, diced

4 sprigs fresh thyme

1 tsp (2 g) ground cloves

¼ cup (60 g) browning seasoning

1 Scotch bonnet pepper

¼ cup (30 g) all-purpose flour

Salt and pepper

2 tbsp (30 ml) hot pepper sauce (optional)

Clean the goat with water and the vinegar, and remove any excess fat. Heat the oil in large pot over medium-high heat, add the goat and brown the meat, about 8 minutes. Add the tomato paste and mix in well. Then add enough water to cover the meat by 2 inches (5 cm). Simmer for 45 minutes, then skim any fat from the surface. Add more water if needed. Cook for another 25 minutes. Skim again. Add the onion, garlic, bell peppers, celery, thyme and cloves to the pot and boil for 30 minutes. Lower the heat to a simmer, then add the browning seasoning and Scotch bonnet pepper. Cover and simmer for another hour.

In a separate bowl, combine the flour and ½ cup (120 ml) of water in a bowl. Stir together until you get a smooth, thick mixture and then add this to the pot. Stir well to fully incorporate into the soup. Remove the Scotch bonnet pepper. Salt and pepper to taste and add the hot pepper sauce, if using. Serve hot. This can be a meal by itself or may be served with rice.

JACKSON CLAN RED PEA SOUP

yield: 8 servings

My dad loves to get the whole family together just to sit around and talk and simply enjoy spending time as a family. Often, when he invites all eight kids and their families over, he makes a big pot of red pea soup for everyone to enjoy. In the Caribbean, "red pea" is slang for "red beans." The key to making red pea soup like a true Virgin Islander is to make it sweet! Something about the sweet broth and the salty pork is an irresistible combination. I have such great memories of sitting around with a bowl of soup, laughing and talking with my brothers and sisters. Now that I have a son of my own, I'm looking forward to sharing these memories with him and I am sure he will love this soup as much as you will!

1 lb (455 g) salted pork pieces, soaked overnight

2 tbsp (30 ml) vegetable oil

1 yellow onion, chopped

1 celery rib, finely chopped

3 cloves garlic, minced

3 sprigs thyme

1 (14-oz [400-g]) can red kidney beans, drained and rinsed

½ cup (100 g) sugar

½ lb (225 g) tannia or taro, peeled and chopped

½ lb (225 g) potatoes, cubed

1 lb (455 g) sweet potatoes, peeled and chopped

2 batches Down Island Dumplings (page 128), cut into 2" (5-cm) pieces

Salt and pepper

Soak the salted pork in cold water overnight in the refrigerator, changing the water once after 2 hours, then let sit. Drain the next day.

In a large soup pot, heat the oil, add the pork, onion, celery, garlic and thyme and sauté over medium-high heat for 7 minutes. Add 12 cups (2.8 L) of water and bring to a boil. Lower the heat to a simmer and cook for 25 minutes, skimming off any foam that forms at the top of the soup. Add the beans, sugar, tannia and potatoes. Simmer for 50 minutes, add the dumplings and cook for 10 minutes more, or until the root vegetables are tender. Salt and pepper to taste.

30-MINUTE BEEF SOUP

Yield: 7 to 9 servings

My wife and I have very different personalities in the kitchen. She looks at leftovers as destined for the trash can. I look at leftovers and see a whole new possibility for tomorrow's dinner. For example, when I have leftover beef from a roast, I like to incorporate it into a light soup that can be made in less than 30 minutes. Because this soup doesn't cook long, make sure to choose a high-quality beef broth as your base.

2 tbsp (30 ml) olive oil

1¼ cups (200 g) chopped onion

2 celery ribs, chopped

1 cup (130 g) diced carrot

2 cloves garlic, minced

3 cups (360 ml) beef stock

Salt

1½ lb (680 g) penne pasta

2 bay leaves

1 cup (130 g) frozen peas

3 tbsp (4 g) dried parsley

2 tbsp (6 g) dried oregano

2 lb (905 g) cubed cooked roast beef

Freshly ground black pepper

In a large pot, heat the oil and sauté the onion, celery, carrot and garlic for 5 minutes over medium heat. Add 4 cups (946 ml) of water, the beef stock and a pinch of salt, then bring to a boil. Once boiling, add the pasta, bay leaves, peas and herbs. Boil for 15 minutes, or until the pasta is tender, then add beef. Turn off the heat and let sit for 5 minutes before serving. Remove the bay leaves and add salt and pepper to taste.

COKI BEACH SEAFOOD KALLALOO

yield: 12 servings

This is a traditional soup that my grandma always made around the holidays. She lived near my favorite beach on St. Thomas, Coki Beach. Many of the men on my mom's side of the family are fishermen, so my grandma's seafood kallaloo was almost always made with fresh snapper that had been caught that same day. Kallaloo is probably my favorite soup and is also extremely popular throughout the Caribbean.

Kallaloo is perfect as an appetizer or pre-dinner soup, but a larger bowl-size serving can also serve as a meal by itself.

1 lb (455 g) salt cod

3 lb (1.4 kg) spinach, well rinsed

1½ lb (680 g) okra

2 lb (905 g) shrimp, cleaned and chopped

1½ lb (680 g) snapper fillets, diced

1 lb (455 g) crab claw meat

1 large onion, diced

2 cloves garlic, minced

5 sprigs thyme, roughly chopped

1 Scotch bonnet pepper

3 tbsp (42 g) unsalted butter

Salt and pepper

Boil the salt cod in 3 quarts (2.8 L) of water for 45 minutes. After boiling, taste the water. If the water is too salty, add 1 more quart (946 ml). Then add all the remaining ingredients, except the butter, salt and pepper. Bring the soup back to a boil. Once the water boils, lower the heat to a simmer and cover. Simmer for another 45 minutes. Finally, add the butter and stir well. Salt and pepper to taste. Remove the Scotch bonnet pepper before serving. This is best when served piping hot!

PORK KALLALOO

yield: 10 servings

Kallaloo is almost always offered up in one of two versions: seafood or pork. The salted pork, as well as the length of cooking time, adds a smoky depth to the kallaloo. When living on an island, one learns to be resourceful and it is not uncommon to see some of the less popular animal parts featured in a recipe. I'll share the secret I have learned—these are the parts that have some of the most flavor.

1 salted ham bone

2 lb (905 g) salted pork, pig's tail, pig's feet, soaked overnight

3 lb (1.4 kg) spinach, well rinsed

1½ lb (680 g) okra

1½ lb (680 g) snapper fillet, diced

1 large onion, diced

2 cloves garlic, minced

5 sprigs thyme, roughly chopped

1 Scotch bonnet pepper

3 tbsp (42 g) unsalted butter

Salt and pepper

Boil the salted ham bone in 3 quarts (2.8 L) of water with the salted pork for 45 minutes. At this point, taste the water to test for saltiness. If the water is too salty, add 1 more quart (946 ml) of water to the pot. Boil until the pork is tender, about 1 hour.

Remove the pork and set aside, but leave the ham bone in the pot. Then add all of the remaining ingredients, except the butter, salt and pepper. Bring the soup to a boil. Once the water boils, lower the heat to a simmer, add the pork back to the pot and simmer, covered, for 45 minutes. Finally, add the butter and stir well. Salt and pepper to taste. Remove the Scotch bonnet pepper before serving hot.

LIGHT AND FIT FISH SOUP

Yield: 10 servings

Typically, I train five days a week in my boxing gym. But Saturdays are always a treat because on Saturday mornings, I do a beach workout. I love my beach workouts because I get to enjoy the beautiful place I live, work out in the water and feel really energized afterward. It's a tough workout, though! Running in the sand is not an easy feat. There is a food truck on the beach that sells an amazing fish soup that I always treat myself to after a workout. I love that it is light and full of vegetables, but so filling. It's a perfect post-workout meal. I loved it so much that I had to re-create it using my own unique recipe. It is my pleasure to share that recipe with you.

2 tbsp (30 ml) vegetable oil

1 large onion, diced

2 large carrots, diced

3 cloves garlic, minced

1 large green bell pepper, diced

1 large red bell pepper, diced

1 celery rib, diced

3 sprigs fresh thyme

1 scallion, diced

3 cups (270 g) cubed white cabbage

8 cups (1.9 L) fish or vegetable stock

3 large tannia or taro, peeled and cubed

3 large potatoes, cubed

1 lb (455 g) calabaza pumpkin, seeded and diced

1 tbsp (4 g) chopped fresh parsley leaves

1 Scotch bonnet pepper

3 lb (1.4 kg) any white fish, filleted but with head, cubed

1 batch Down Island Dumplings (page 128), cut into ½" (1.3-cm) pieces

Salt and pepper

In large soup pot, heat the oil over medium-high heat, then add the onion, carrots, garlic, bell peppers, celery, thyme, scallions and cabbage. Sauté the vegetables for 5 minutes, then add the stock and 10 to 12 cups (2.4 to 2.8 L) of water. Once the water starts to boil, add the tannia, potatoes, pumpkin, parsley, Scotch bonnet pepper and fish. Cover, lower the heat and simmer for 30 minutes, or until the potatoes are soft. Add the dumpling dough and cook for 15 more minutes. Depending on your preference, remove the fish head and Scotch bonnet pepper before serving. Add salt and pepper to taste, then enjoy hot!

EASY WEEKNIGHT PIGEON PEA SOUP

yield: 8 servings

This soup has the consistency of a lentil soup and is brimming with vegetables. This soup's flavors develop naturally from the peas and the vegetables, so no broth is needed. That's handy for me when I'm hankering for soup, though may be missing ingredients for others, I almost always have the ingredients for this soup on hand! While I have included many fresh, local ingredients, this recipe can easily be made with whatever you have on hand. It can easily be made vegetarian by omitting the pork.

½ lb (225 g) pig's tail (optional)

½ lb (225 g) pig's feet (optional)

1 tbsp (15 ml) olive oil

1 large yellow onion, chopped

1 large carrot, peeled and diced

2 celery ribs, chopped

2 (15-oz [425-g]) cans pigeon peas, drained and rinsed

1 Scotch bonnet pepper

1 large sweet potato, peeled and diced

½ lb (225 g) calabaza pumpkin, peeled, seeded and diced

1 large potato, peeled and diced

2 sprigs thyme

2 cloves garlic, minced

1 tomato, diced

1 tbsp (16 g) tomato paste

1 batch Down Island Dumpling dough (page 128)

Salt and pepper

If using the optional pig's tail and feet, begin by boiling them in 8 cups (1.9 L) of water for 30 minutes.

In a large pot, heat the olive oil over medium-high heat, then sauté the onion, carrot and celery for 5 minutes. Next, add the pigeon peas to the pot and lower to a simmer. Add the remaining ingredients, except the dumplings, salt and pepper, and simmer, covered, for 35 minutes, or until the potatoes are tender. Add the dumplings and cook for 10 more minutes. Remove the Scotch bonnet pepper and add salt and black pepper to taste. Serve hot.

Satisfying Snacks and Sides

You might think of a meal with three parts: starch, protein and vegetable (and dessert, if you're lucky). Here in the Caribbean, we do things a little differently! We love our side dishes, and often don't feel as if a meal is complete without many options for starches. A full, colorful plate packed with flavor always makes us smile. We also love to snack! My mom will often whip up something in the kitchen outside of mealtime. It's one more way to bring the family together and feed the soul along with the body. Try one of these standout snacks or sides to make your meal feel complete!

DAWN'S COAL POT SALTFISH CAKES

yield: 10 servings

I am blessed to be surrounded by some truly amazing cooks. My mother-in-law is one of the finest cooks I know and she loves to cook elaborate, multi-course meals when all six of her children and their families gather in St. Thomas. Normally, the cooking happens at our house, so I've been able to observe and learn from her over the years. One year, she even convinced me to compete in the first annual local coal pot cooking competition held in downtown Charlotte Amalie as a fundraiser for the St. Thomas Historical Trust. We ended up taking home first prize and these saltfish cakes were our most popular item by far. We couldn't get them out of the coal pot fast enough to keep the attendees satisfied and our booth had the longest line, with many people patiently waiting to sample one of these tasty treats.

1 lb (455 g) boneless salt cod

1½ tsp (7.5 ml) olive oil

½ yellow onion, diced

1 celery rib, diced

1 sprig parsley, chopped

1 sprig thyme, chopped

¼ cup (60 ml) tomato sauce

⅔ cup (83 g) all-purpose flour

⅓ cup (43 g) white whole wheat flour

1½ tsp (7 g) baking powder

½ tsp freshly ground black pepper

1 large egg

½ cup (120 ml) whole milk

2 cups (455 ml) vegetable oil

First, soak the salt cod overnight, changing the water twice. The next day, place the cod in a large pot and cover with water, then boil the fish for 10 minutes. Next, drain the fish and allow to cool for 10 minutes. Once cooled, shred the fish with a fork and be sure to remove any bones.

When ready to cook, in a medium skillet, heat the olive oil over medium-high heat and then sauté the onion, celery, parsley and thyme for 5 minutes. Add the tomato sauce to the pan and sauté for another 5 minutes, then remove from the heat.

While the vegetables cook, in a large mixing bowl, combine the flours, baking powder and pepper and mix well until evenly distributed. In a small bowl, beat the egg and the milk together until combined. Add the milk mixture, vegetables and saltfish to the flour mixture and mix everything together until fully incorporated.

To fry the saltfish cakes, heat the vegetable oil in a deep skillet over medium-high heat. Cook the cakes by dropping the dough by the tablespoon (15 g) into the hot oil. Cook for about 4 minutes, or until the cakes are golden brown, then flip and cook for an additional 4 minutes.

BALLPARK-STYLE JOHNNY-CAKES AND FRIED CHICKEN

yield: 14 servings

Growing up in Las Vegas during the height of my father's boxing career, the family often attended many different sporting events. Popcorn and hot dogs were on every menu. In the Virgin Islands, when you go to a ball game or other sporting event, you can count on a meal of fried chicken legs and johnnycakes. Johnnycakes are probably most similar to a funnel cake, except that they have a different shape and are not as sweet. What they are is delicious fried dough served as a side dish, which pairs well with almost anything in this book! Throughout the Caribbean, johnnycakes go by many names. In Trinidad for example, they call them bakes. There's much discussion about whether to make 1- to 2-inch (2.5- to 5-cm) slits in the johnnycakes. The purpose of the slits is unknown to me. What I do know is that, in the Virgin Islands, we add slits to our johnnycake, and I plan to stay true to that tradition in this recipe.

Johnnycakes

10 cups (1.25 kg) all-purpose flour, plus more for dusting

10 tsp (46 g) baking powder

5 tsp (30 g) salt

1 cup (200 g) sugar

¼ cup (60 ml) vegetable oil

Fried Chicken

14 chicken drumsticks

3 oz (85 ml) vinegar

3 tbsp (40 g) all purpose seasoning

1 tbsp (15 g) black pepper

1 tbsp (15 g) onion powder

8 cups (1.8 L) vegetable oil

Ketchup (optional)

To make the jonnycakes: In a large bowl, mix together the flour, baking powder, salt and sugar. Using a spatula, pat the dry mixture toward the sides of the bowl to create a well in the center. Add about 5 cups (1.2 L) of water and the oil in the center and fold the wet into the dry until you have a soft, sticky dough. Let the dough sit for 5 minutes, then remove from the bowl and place on a well-floured surface. Sprinkle a bit of extra flour over the dough (enough to cover the top) and knead until smooth.

Shape the dough into 3-inch (7.5-cm) balls. Flatten the dough balls with a rolling pin, then, using a knife, put two parallel 1- to 2-inch (2.5- to 5-cm) slits in the center (you do not want to cut completely through the dough). In a deep skillet, heat the oil until hot and fry the dough until the underside is golden brown. Flip, then cook until the second side is also golden brown.

To make the fried chicken: First, place the chicken in a large container with enough water to cover it. Add the vinegar and soak for 10 minutes.

Strain the drumsticks, removing as much liquid as possible. Mix the all purpose seasoning, black pepper and onion powder together and then season the drumsticks with it.

In a medium-sized deep pot, heat the vegetable oil over medium heat until it reaches 365°F (185°C). Fry the drumsticks in batches of 4, for 10 to 15 minutes, or until crispy and dark golden brown. Remove from the fryer and let cool on a paper towel–lined plate. Serve with a johnnycake and ketchup (if using) for dipping.

CARNIVAL BEEF PATE
yield: 11 servings

As you travel throughout the Caribbean, you'll see the paté called by many different names, such as a patty, empanada or *pastelito*. Essentially, it is fried dough with various types of filling. Most home cooks only make patés for special occasions or on the weekends because of the need to stand at the oven and fry each paté individually. But they are extremely popular at our local Carnival Village and street fairs because they are so easy to eat while strolling around and socializing. These are sure to be a hit at parties!

2 lb (905 g) lean ground beef

2 yellow onions, diced

1 celery rib, diced

6 cloves garlic, minced

1 green bell pepper, diced

1 red bell pepper, diced

3 tbsp (48 g) tomato paste

2 tsp (10 g) all-purpose seasoning

¼ Scotch bonnet pepper, minced

5 sprigs thyme, minced

Salt and pepper

½ batch Johnnycake dough (page 103)

All-purpose flour, for dusting (optional)

8 cups (1.9 L) vegetable oil

In a large skillet, brown the ground beef over medium heat. With a ladle, remove some of the excess fat from the pan and discard. Then add all the vegetables, tomato paste, all-purpose seasoning, Scotch bonnet pepper and thyme to the pan, stirring well to incorporate the tomato paste throughout the mixture. Cook for an additional 15 minutes. Salt and pepper to taste, then remove from the heat and set aside.

To assemble, if the johnnycake dough was frozen, defrost it to room temperature. Take half of your prepared johnnycake dough and roll it out as thinly as possible (about 1⁄16 inch [2 mm]) on a floured surface or parchment paper. Next, using a small bowl, cut 6-inch (15-cm) circles from the dough. In the center of each piece of dough, place a rounded ½-cup (85-g) mound of the meat mixture. Bring opposite edges of the dough to meet each other around the meat mixture to form a semicircle. Seal the rounded edges of the dough, pressing them firmly together with a fork. Repeat with the rest of the dough and filling. In a deep skillet, heat the vegetable oil to 360°F (182°C). Fry the patés until golden brown, about 7 minutes on each side. Serve hot.

SALTFISH PATÉ

yield: 12 servings

For a pescatarian take on the paté, we fill it with saltfish. The saltiness of the filling is the perfect balance to the surrounding dough. They're sure to please those seafood lovers in your life.

2 lb (905 g) salt cod

2 tbsp (27 g) unsalted butter

2 yellow onions, diced

1 red bell pepper, diced

1 green bell pepper, diced

3 cloves garlic, minced

1 celery rib, diced

4 sprigs thyme, minced

2 tbsp (32 g) tomato paste

¼ Scotch bonnet pepper, minced

Salt and pepper

½ batch Johnnycake dough
(page 103)

All-purpose flour, for dusting
(optional)

8 cups (1.9 L) vegetable oil

Soak the salt cod in water overnight or for at least 8 hours, changing the water at least once after a minimum of 2 hours. Do not soak the cod for longer than 12 hours. After the cod is finished soaking, drain and place in a pot of fresh water. Boil the cod for 15 minutes. Drain, then shred with a fork and set aside.

Heat a large sauté pan over high heat and add butter. Once the butter has melted, add the onions, bell peppers, garlic, celery and thyme. Sauté for 7 minutes, then lower the heat to medium. Add the tomato paste, Scotch bonnet pepper and cod, mix well and cook for additional 10 minutes. Salt and pepper to taste.

To assemble, if the johnnycake dough was frozen, defrost it to room temperature. Take half of your prepared johnnycake dough and roll it out as thin as possible (about ¹⁄₁₆ inch [2 mm]) on a floured surface or parchment paper. Next, using a small bowl, cut 6-inch (15-cm) circles from the dough. In the center of each piece of dough, place a rounded ½-cup (85-g) mound of the saltfish mixture. Bring the two pieces of the dough to meet each other around the fish mixture to form a semicircle. Seal the rounded edges of the dough, pressing them firmly together with a fork. Repeat with the remaining dough and filling. In a deep skillet, heat the vegetable oil to 360°F (182°C). Fry the patés until golden brown, about 7 minutes on each side. Serve hot.

LOBSTER PATÉ

yield: 12 servings

The differences between a New England lobster and a Caribbean lobster are quite distinct. Caribbean lobsters are smaller and taste more salty than sweet, as compared to their northern counterparts. Personally, I've always preferred Caribbean lobster, no surprise there. I know a number of local fishermen and I love when I can score some fresh lobster from them! The key with lobster is that it must be cooked right away to be preserved. So even if you don't plan to use it in a meal right away, it must be boiled before you can refrigerate it for any length of time. Using lobster in a paté is a great way to elevate this humble dish into something gourmet. The simple dough allows the lobster to be the star of the show. This is an indulgence I almost never turn down!

2 lb 2 oz (960 g) fresh Caribbean or ordinary lobster tails

2 tbsp (28 g) unsalted butter

1 green bell pepper, julienned

1 red bell pepper, julienned

2 red onions, julienned

1 celery rib, julienned

2 cloves garlic, minced

1 tomato, diced

1 (14-oz [400-g]) can stewed tomatoes

4 sprigs thyme, diced

Salt and pepper

½ batch Johnnycake dough (page 103)

All-purpose flour, for dusting (optional)

8 cups (1.9 L) vegetable oil

In a large pot, bring to a boil enough water to completely submerge the lobster tails, and cook for 20 minutes. Drain and let cool for about 20 minutes. With a sharp knife, cut each tail in half and remove the meat. Dice into small chunks and set aside.

In a large sauté pan, heat the butter over medium-high heat. Once the butter has melted, add the peppers, onions, celery and garlic, then sauté for 5 minutes. Next, add the tomato, stewed tomatoes and thyme and sauté for an additional 2 minutes. Finally, add the lobster meat and turn off the heat, mixing the lobster in to incorporate well. Salt and pepper to taste.

To assemble, if the johnnycake dough was frozen, defrost it to room temperature. Take half of your prepared johnnycake dough and roll it out as thinly as possible (about ¹⁄₁₆ inch [2 mm]) on a floured surface or parchment paper. Next, using a small bowl, cut 6-inch (15-cm) circles out of the dough. In the center of each piece of dough, place a ½-cup (85-g) mound of the lobster mixture. Bring two opposite edges of the dough to meet each other around the lobster mixture to form a semicircle. Seal the rounded edges of the dough, pressing them firmly together with a fork. In a deep skillet, heat the vegetable oil to 360°F (182°C). Fry the patés until golden brown, about 7 minutes on each side. Serve hot.

TOSTONES

yield: 1 servings

Tostones are a popular side dish in Latin American cooking, especially in Puerto Rican and Dominican Republic cultures. They get their name from the cooking preparation, which requires a green, unripe plantain to be fried twice. Many Latin American cooks have a tostonera, a special hinged tool used to flatten the plantain after the first fry. However, the plantains can also be flattened with a glass cup or the bottom of a mortar (or really any heavy, flat object you have in your kitchen). The crunch and saltiness of tostones make it hard to eat just one!

---

2 green plantains
¼ cup (60 ml) vegetable oil
Salt

Using a paring knife, peel the skin off the plantains. The easiest way is to make a long vertical cut in a plantain, then cut off each end and peel the skin away. Cut the plantain on a diagonal angle into 1-inch (2.5-cm)-thick slices.

In a large skillet, heat the oil over medium heat for 4 to 5 minutes. To check whether the oil is at the proper temperature, use one plantain as a tester. Fry all the slices from one plantain until soft and pale yellow, 2 to 3 minutes per side (note: not until golden brown; you want to remove them from the pan before this). Because different parts of the pan heat differently, you will base cooking on softness, not on time. Remove from the pan and while the plantain slices are still warm, flatten them with bottom of mortar, glass cup, plate or another large, flat surface.

Return the flattened plantains to the frying oil and fry until golden brown, 1 to 2 minutes per side. Transfer to a paper towel to absorb the excess oil. Repeat to fry and drain the remaining sliced plantain and add salt to taste while the plantains are still hot. These are best served right away from the pan and lose their crunch as time passes.

PANFRIED BREADFRUIT

yield: 15 servings

I'm fortunate that my property in St. Thomas is filled with local fruits and vegetables. One of the most fruitful trees is our breadfruit tree. Breadfruit is naturally a bit sweet and has the consistency of a root vegetable. For a few years, our driveway was covered in breadfruit. Surprisingly, my neighbors rarely wanted to share in the bounty, and we always seemed to have an excess of breadfruit that would be wasted. So seeing this, I started experimenting with different ways to prepare a breadfruit to ensure that we wouldn't lose a single one! Traditional preparation of breadfruit involves boiling and sprinkling a bit of salt. Inspired by how enjoyable plantains are with a quick frying, I tried that with the breadfruit and the result was scrumptious. This dish is a little salty, a little sweet, mostly crunchy and totally delicious!

1 whole ripe breadfruit

1 tbsp (45 ml) olive oil

Salt and pepper

Preheat the oven to 325°F (170°C). Wash the breadfruit thoroughly and dry well. Wrap the breadfruit in foil, place in the oven and bake for 20 minutes.

Remove the breadfruit from the oven and let cool. Peel the breadfruit and cut off the stem. Next, cut the breadfruit meat into large pieces. The shape isn't important, so use any shape you like. I normally cut the breadfruit into triangles.

In a skillet, heat the oil over medium-high heat. Fry the breadfruit pieces until golden brown, 2 to 3 minutes on each side. Transfer the fried breadfruit to a paper towel–lined plate to absorb any excess oil. Sprinkle salt and pepper to taste over the breadfruit and eat it hot!

PANFRIED PLANTAINS

yield: 9 servings

Fried ripe plantain is the perfect sweet accompaniment to any dish in this book. I find that when you add a side of plantains to a meal, it serves as a palate cleanser between bites of otherwise heavy foods. The crispy, sweet treat is also a great snack on its own. These are best eaten just a few minutes after cooking, while they are still hot. The ideal plantains to use in this recipe are yellow ones that have already started to get some brown or black spots.

4 very ripe plantains
½ cup (120 ml) vegetable oil
Salt

To peel the plantains, cut off each end, then run your knife in a shallow cut vertically down the edge to create an opening. The skin should now easily peel away from the fruit. Next, cut the fruit diagonally into 1-inch strips. In a skillet, heat the oil over medium-high heat. Depending on the size of your pan, add 4 or 5 plantain slices at a time. Fry the pieces until dark golden brown, 2 to 3 minutes on each side. Remove the plantain slices from the pan and place on a paper towel–lined plate to absorb any excess oil. Repeat until all the plantain strips are fried. Sprinkle salt to taste over the plantains and eat after they have cooled for 1 to 2 minutes.

GRANNY'S POTATO STUFFING

yield: 12 servings

This is a traditional side dish that is eaten at almost every party or holiday celebration. Potato stuffing is orange in color, so many people assume it is made from sweet potatoes, but it is actually made from regular white potatoes and the orange color comes from tomato paste. It has a slightly sweet taste to it, but its consistency is like that of mashed potatoes.

Living in the Virgin Islands, most people will tell you that they learned how to cook local recipes from their grandparents. This is one of my wife's favorite foods and this recipe was handed down from her grandmother; hence Granny's Potato Stuffing. Try making it for your Thanksgiving celebration this year, to give your table a VI twist!

2 lb (905 g) potatoes, peeled

¼ cup (60 ml) olive oil

¼ small red bell pepper, finely chopped

1 small, fresh tomato, finely chopped

1 medium onion, finely chopped

½ celery rib (including leaves), finely chopped

2 cloves garlic, finely chopped

½ cup plus 2 tbsp (4.5 oz [160 g]) tomato paste (from a 6-oz [170-g] can)

1 (4-oz [115-g]) box raisins (optional)

1 tbsp (13 g) sugar

1½ tsp (8 ml) hot pepper sauce (optional)

Preheat the oven to 350°F (180°C). In a pot on the stovetop, boil the potatoes for 25 minutes, then mash them. In a medium saucepan, heat the oil, add the chopped bell pepper, tomato, onion, celery and garlic and cook over medium-high heat until softened, about 3 minutes. Add the tomato paste and raisins, if using, to the pan and cook for 2 minutes. Transfer the chopped vegetable mixture to the potato mixture and mix until it is a homogenous orange color. Add the sugar and hot sauce, if using, and mix until the sugar is no longer visible. Spoon the mixture into an oven-safe baking dish and bake for 30 minutes.

BEST-EVER BAKED MACARONI AND CHEESE

yield: 10 servings

Macaroni and cheese is a popular dish around the United States, but I happen to think no one does it like us in the Caribbean. Our baked macaroni and cheese has a crispy, crunchy top and is still creamy and smooth in the middle. What's great about this recipe is that any leftovers can be frozen and used over time as a side dish. Serve this with barbecue or stewed chicken when you need some real comfort food.

1 tbsp (14 g) unsalted butter, plus more for baking dish

1 tbsp (18 g) salt

2 tbsp (30 ml) olive oil

1 (8-oz [225-g]) package elbow macaroni pasta

2 tbsp (15 g) all-purpose flour

1½ cups (355 ml) whole milk, divided

1 large egg, beaten

12 oz (340 g) cheddar cheese, shredded or grated, divided

Preheat the oven to 375°F (190°C). Grease a 10 x 12 x 2½-inch (25.5 x 30.5 x 6.5-cm) baking dish with butter.

In a large pot, bring water plus the salt and oil to a boil. Add the macaroni and cook until a tender al dente. Drain the macaroni and set aside.

In small cup or bowl, whisk the flour and ½ cup (120 ml) of the milk until smooth.

In medium pot over low heat, combine the remaining cup (235 ml) of milk and the tablespoon (14 g) of butter, egg, 10 ounces (280 g) of the cheese and the flour mixture. Stir until the cheese melts, then pour the cooked macaroni into the cheese mixture. Stir, then pour into the lightly greased baking dish. Sprinkle the reserved 2 ounces (60 g) of cheddar evenly on top.

Bake until lightly toasted on top, 20 to 30 minutes.

SEASIDE SEASONED RICE

yield: 10 servings

Rice is a Caribbean staple and an accompaniment to almost every meal. Any restaurant you visit will have two options: steamed white rice or seasoned rice. I prefer seasoned rice with my dishes because I like to maximize flavor in all aspects of my meal. This rice is simple to prepare and adds an extra boost to meals that need a bit of sprucing up!

2 tbsp (28 g) unsalted butter

1 green bell pepper, diced

1 red bell pepper, diced

1 yellow onion, diced

2 cloves garlic, diced

3 sprigs thyme

1 tbsp (16 g) tomato paste

½ cup (120 ml) tomato sauce

2 tsp (5 g) ground turmeric

2 bay leaves

4 cups (840 g) uncooked white rice

Salt and pepper

Heat a large pot over medium-high heat, melt the butter, and add the bell peppers, onion, garlic and thyme and sauté for 5 minutes. Then add tomato paste, tomato sauce, turmeric and bay leaves and sauté for an additional 5 minutes. Add the rice to the pot and mix well until the rice takes on a reddish color. Add 7 cups (1.7 L) of water and bring to a boil, then lower the heat to a simmer. Cover the pot and cook the rice for another 15 to 20 minutes, or until the water is absorbed. Add salt and pepper to taste. Remove the bay leaves before serving.

PIGEON PEAS AND RICE

Yield: 9 servings

Pigeon peas and rice is a common side to almost any dish. It's like a blank canvas ready to take on the delicious gravy of whatever you serve it with—"As Seen on TV" Caribbean Stewed Chicken (page 35) or No-Mess Curry Chicken (page 40), Must-Have Conch in Butter Sauce (page 44) or Tangy Creole Fish (page 47). It's popular among many of the Caribbean islands.

1 tsp (5 ml) olive oil

1 small onion, diced

1 small red bell pepper, diced

1 small green bell pepper, diced

2 cloves garlic, minced

2 tbsp (32 g) tomato paste

1 tbsp (10 g) Sazón con Azafran

2 cups (420 g) uncooked white rice

1 cup (235 ml) chicken stock

1 (15-oz [425-g]) can pigeon peas, drained and rinsed

1 tbsp (3 g) chopped fresh thyme

1 tbsp (4 g) chopped fresh parsley

Salt and pepper

In a medium pot, heat the oil, then add the onion, bell peppers and garlic. Sauté over medium-high heat until the onion is translucent. Then add the tomato paste, Sazón and rice and stir together well. Add 1½ cups (355 ml) of water and the chicken stock, then the pigeon peas, thyme and parsley, and gently mix. Cover and bring to a boil, then lower the heat to a simmer and cook for 10 minutes, covered. Then turn off the heat, remove the cover and let the steam evaporate. Let the rice sit for 5 minutes before serving. Add salt and pepper taste.

ROCK CITY RED BEANS AND RICE

yield: 10 servings

This recipe is another that my stepmother frequently makes. The addition of cinnamon adds a subtle sweetness to the rice without an overpowering cinnamon flavor. While this dish pairs well with anything, I think it goes especially well with poultry dishes, such as Baby's Favorite Baked Chicken (page 36)! St. Thomas's nickname, Rock City, is the namesake of this recipe.

4 cups (946 ml) coconut milk

1 tsp (2 g) ground cinnamon

2 cloves garlic, minced

2 tsp (9 g) sugar

Salt

4 cups (840 g) uncooked white rice

3 sprigs thyme

2 (15-oz [425-g]) cans red kidney beans, drained and rinsed

Freshly ground black pepper

In a large pot, combine 4 cups (946 ml) of water and the coconut milk, cinnamon, garlic, sugar and a pinch of salt and bring to a boil. Then add the rice, thyme and beans and stir together well. Lower the heat to a simmer, then cover and cook for 20 minutes, or until the liquid is completely evaporated. Add salt and pepper to taste.

Fish and _____. Ask any Virgin Islander to complete this sentence and there is only one thing that makes sense. Fish and fungi (pronounced foon-jee). The perfect pairing.

Fungi is the Caribbean twist on polenta and almost always accompanies seafood dishes. You would be hard pressed to find a local restaurant that served fish and didn't have fungi on the menu. The fungi sops up all the delicious gravy served with your seafood and has that melt-in-your-mouth consistency. It can be paired with Must-Have Conch in Butter Sauce (page 44), Tangy Creole Fish (page 47) or sometimes even "As Seen on TV" Caribbean Stewed Chicken (page 35).

FUNGI

yield: 8 servings

5 oz (140 g) fresh or frozen cut okra

1 tsp (6 g) salt, plus more for serving

1½ cups (210 g) yellow cornmeal

¼ cup (55 g) unsalted butter (½ stick)

Freshly ground black pepper

Bring 2½ cups (590 ml) of water to a boil in a large pot. Place the okra and salt in the boiling water. Let cook for 2 minutes. Slowly add the yellow cornmeal while stirring it in with a fork or a whisk. The mixture will become very thick as you add the cornmeal to the water. Lower the heat to low after all the cornmeal has been added and continue to stir until all lumps are gone. Add water at the end if a thinner consistency is desired. Then add the butter, stir in very well and add salt and pepper to taste. Serve hot!

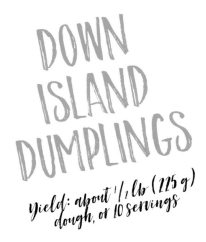

DOWN ISLAND DUMPLINGS

Yield: about ½ lb (225 g) dough, or 10 servings

Dumplings find their way into plenty of dishes, but mostly are a texturally-distinct addition to soups. When buying soup from a restaurant or local soup sale, Caribbean people are quick to make sure their bowl of soup has sufficient dumplings. Less than three in a bowl just isn't acceptable. Dumplings are also commonly served with fish (see recipe on page 95).

2 cups (250 g) all-purpose flour

1 tsp (6 g) salt

1 tbsp (15 ml) vegetable oil

In a bowl, stir together the flour and salt until fully incorporated. Add ⅜ cup (90 ml) of water and the vegetable oil. Keeping the dough in the bowl, knead until the dough is firm and no longer wet (up to 15 minutes). After kneading, roll the dough into an 18-inch (45.5-cm) log, then cut into ½-inch (1.3-cm) pieces. Place in boiling soup or boiling salted water. Cook for 10 minutes. Serve hot!

CREOLE SAUCE

yield: 9 servings

If you're looking for a versatile sauce that you can whip up quickly, is healthy and pairs well with almost any lean protein, this is it! Creole sauce is a tomato-based gravy that is most often served with poultry or seafood. The sauce is made using lots of fresh ingredients and can brighten up an otherwise bland dish.

1 tbsp (15 ml) olive oil

1 large onion, julienned

1 large green bell pepper, julienned

1 large red bell pepper, julienned

2 cloves garlic, minced

1 cup (180 g) roughly chopped tomatoes

1 (8-oz [225-g]) can tomato sauce

½ cup (120 ml) white distilled vinegar

3 bay leaves

3 sprigs thyme

Salt and pepper

In a deep skillet, heat the oil and sauté the onion, bell peppers and garlic over high heat for 2 minutes. Add the tomatoes, tomato sauce, vinegar, bay leaves and thyme and mix well. Bring to a simmer, then cover and let cook for 15 minutes. Remove the bay leaves and salt and pepper to taste. Serve hot.

Vacation in a Glass

In the Caribbean, our climate is hot all year-round. Staying hydrated is always a priority or else you run out of steam before the day is even done. Water and coconut water are our basic choices for hydration, but over the years we've come up with creative ways of infusing our locally grown fruits and plant life into our water. Mango, passion fruit and lemongrass are just a few that have been used in these delicious concoctions. In addition to providing hydration, these drinks are guaranteed to stir up a good time!

TAMARIND JUICE

yield: 1 servings

Tamarind (pronounced tal-mon in the Virgin Islands) has grown in popularity, but it has long been known to Caribbean people—especially those with a sweet tooth. Tamarind is most popularly served as tamarind balls (small balls of sugar-filled pulp), tamarind stew (a jam of sorts that includes the whole seed with some pulp), tamarind "specials" (the VI term for an ice pop, served in a cup), or my personal favorite—tamarind juice. Its taste is both sour and sweet at the same time. Done properly, this juice will give you just the right pucker. Because tamarind takes a while to shell, it is normally reserved for special occasions. One of those occasions is the carnival celebration in the Virgin Islands. Carnival consists of about one month of activities, including a parade, a queen selection pageant, children's rides and a food fair. The food fair is one of the places you are guaranteed to find various tamarind delicacies.

About 20 ripe tamarinds, shelled

5 tbsp (65 g) sugar

Bring 6 cups (1.4 L) of water to a boil. Place the shelled tamarinds in a large, heatproof glass container and add the boiling water. Let sit for 50 minutes. Over a large metal bowl, pour the liquid and tamarind pulp through a fine sifter or sieve, while stirring vigorously to get pulp off the tamarind seeds. Add the sugar to the strained liquid and stir well until the sugar is no longer visible. Serve chilled, or freeze in a cup for a delicious Virgin Islands specialty!

SORREL

yield: 10 servings

This drink, made from the flower petals of the sorrel plant, is one of my absolute favorites. It is so aromatic, flavorful and refreshing. There are few things more relaxing than sipping a glass of Sorrel over ice on a hot day. Because the Sorrel on its own has so much flavor, you really don't need to add much sugar to this drink, which makes it a perfect low-calorie option for your mimosa bar!

½ cup (116 g) dried sorrel petals

1 tbsp (8 g) grated fresh ginger

½ large lemon, sliced

1 tsp (2 g) whole cloves

½ cinnamon stick

1 tsp (5 ml) vanilla extract

1½ to 3 cups (300 to 600 g) sugar

To begin, bring 2 quarts (1.9 L) of water to a boil. Then remove from the heat and let cool for a few minutes while you assemble the rest of the ingredients.

In a large, sealable glass container, combine the sorrel petals, ginger, lemon slices, cloves and cinnamon stick. Pour the hot water over the mixture. Let the mixture sit overnight or for at least 8 hours at room temperature in the sealed container.

After the mixture sits, stir the ingredients with a whisk or long fork, pressing them against the side of the container to extract the maximum flavor. Next, pour the mixture through a fine strainer into a large pitcher and discard the solids. Add the vanilla and the sugar to your liking; I recommended you start with 1½ cups (300 g) of sugar. Some people enjoy this warm or at room temperature, but I suggest it served over ice!

SORREL MANGO DRINK

yield: 20 servings

At first glance, sorrel and mango don't seem like a likely combination. Sorrel is very light and creates a mild, gentle flavor, whereas mango is pulpy and sweet. But when these two mix together, they create a complementary balance, resulting in a sweet, vibrantly colored and very smooth beverage. A must-try!

2 whole mangoes, sliced (reserve the seed)

1½ cups (200 g) dried sorrel leaves

½ large lemon, sliced

1 tbsp (8 g) grated fresh ginger

1 tsp (2 g) whole cloves

½ cinnamon stick

1 tsp (5 ml) vanilla extract

1 cup (200 g) sugar

In a large pot, combine 2 quarts (1.9 L) of water and the mango slices and its seed. Bring to a boil, boil for 3 minutes, then remove from the heat. Cover and let the mixture cool for 10 minutes. While still warm, transfer the mango water to a large glass container, then add the sorrel leaves, lemon slices, ginger, cloves and cinnamon stick. Let the mixture steep overnight or for at least 8 hours in the refrigerator.

Strain the liquid into a large pitcher and add the vanilla and sugar. Serve chilled.

HOME-GROWN LIMEADE

yield: 4 servings

When I was a child, my dad liked to grow fruits in our yard and was very interested in introducing new fruit trees on the property. One time in particular, I remember his cutting open a lime and wondering whether the seeds would grow in our soil. To satisfy his curiosity my dad and older brother buried those lime seeds right beyond our chicken coop. From those seeds, we were able to grow a lot of limes. One hot day, we ran out of Kool-Aid and were craving something sweet to drink. Pops said, "Let's make lemonade with the limes!" He said he used to drink this quite a bit as a kid. This seemed weird to us, but we did it anyway. The "limeade" was amazing! I am now proud to share this recipe with you, so that your family can also enjoy this delicious and refreshing drink.

¼ cup (50 g) sugar

6 limes

1 tsp (5 ml) vanilla extract

In a medium pot, combine 3 cups (710 ml) of water and the sugar and bring to a boil. Remove from the heat and let cool. Cut the limes in half and squeeze their juice into water over a strainer to catch the seeds, also adding the lime halves after squeezing. Then add the vanilla and stir well. Serve chilled or over ice.

FRESH-OFF-THE-TREE PASSION FRUIT JUICE

Yield: 10 servings

When I was a kid, I never saw passion fruit juice sold in the store year-round. It was only served during passion fruit season when the fruits were falling plentifully from the vines. Nowadays, I see many passion fruit juice products on the shelves, and to be honest, I haven't tasted any product that comes anywhere near the genuine flavor of fresh passion fruit. That tart, tangy passion fruit flavor is best when homemade. The key to making this juice is to be sure the water is hot enough so that the pulp separates easily from the seed. If you like things a bit on the sour side, cut back on the sugar, but I personally like it sweet.

2 cups (290 g) passion fruit pulp (from 18 to 20 whole passion fruits)

2 cups (400 g) sugar, or to taste

To begin, bring 2 quarts (1.9 L) of water to a boil, remove from the heat and let cool for 3 minutes. Place the passion fruit pulp in a large container and add the water. Let the mixture sit overnight in the refrigerator or for at least 8 hours.

After the mixture sits, stir the pulp with a whisk or long fork, pressing it against the side of the container to extract the maximum flavor. Next, pour the mixture through a fine strainer into a large pitcher and discard the pulp. Add sugar to your liking; I recommended you start with 2 cups (400 g).

PASSIONATE PAPAYA MIX-UP

yield: 10 servings

It sometimes surprises me that I grew up to be such a food lover when I grew up with some very picky eaters for brothers. My one brother, Julian Jr., even refuses to ever in his life eat a banana, if you can believe that. Needless to say, neither of them has ever been a fan of papaya. This juice makes even people who don't like papaya lick their lips in satisfaction. The papaya tree is extremely resilient, able to withstand hurricanes and harsh weather conditions. I have at least ten papaya trees in my yard and once papaya season rolls around, I have more papayas than I know what to do with. In turn, I make juice and will often give it away to family members . . . even the ones who don't know they are drinking papaya! Papaya has received much acclaim for having many health benefits, so I like to think I am doing them a favor.

2 cups (290 g) passion fruit pulp (from 18 to 20 whole passion fruits)

1 cup (145 g) papaya pulp (very ripe)

2¼ cups (450 g) sugar, or to taste

To begin, boil 2 quarts (1.9 L) of water. Once it has come to a boil, remove from the heat and let cool for 3 minutes. Place the passion fruit pulp in a large container and pour in the hot water. Let the mixture sit overnight in the refrigerator or for at least 8 hours.

After the mixture sits, stir the passionfruit pulp with a whisk or long fork, pressing it against the side of the pitcher to extract the maximum flavor. Next, pour the mixture through a fine strainer into a large pitcher and discard the passion fruit pulp. Pour the strained liquid into a blender and add the papaya pulp plus sugar to your liking; I recommend you start with 2¼ cups (450 g). Blend. Serve chilled. Natural separation will occur and you will need to stir before serving once it has settled.

TROPICAL FRUIT PUNCH

yield: 5 servings

After a hot day at the gym, I feel as if I can drink a whole gallon (3.8 L) of juice. Sometimes, I even do. Not only is this fruit punch tasty, but it is also another quintessential VI recipe. There isn't a restaurant on St. Thomas that doesn't have fruit punch on the menu and almost everyone makes it in-house. I've probably sampled them all, ha!

8 oz (235 ml) pineapple juice

8 oz (235 ml) freshly squeezed orange juice

4 oz (120 ml) guava juice

3 oz (90 ml) grenadine

4 oz (120 ml) passion fruit juice

Juice of 1 lemon

Place all the ingredients in large container and stir together. Serve cold or over ice.

NOT YOUR RESORT'S PIÑA COLADA

yield: 6 servings

A frozen piña colada on a hot day in August or September is one of life's simple pleasures that truly feels like an indulgence. Most resorts or restaurants you dine at use pre-made mixes so as to make drinks quickly and cheaply. However, making a fresh piña colada can also be quick. These ingredients are available year-round in your grocery store. So, the next time you are jonesing for a Caribbean vacation, whip up one of these instead.

2 cups (330 g) fresh pineapple chunks

½ cup (120 ml) pineapple juice

½ cup (120 ml) cream of coconut

1½ cups (355 g) crushed ice

¼ cup (60 g) fresh young coconut jelly (optional, but highly recommended if you can find it)

Combine all the ingredients in a blender and blend for 2 to 3 minutes, or until smooth. Pour into your favorite cocktail cups and garnish with a wedge of fresh pineapple.

LEMONGRASS TEA TO THE RESCUE

Yield: 8 servings

Homemade remedies for common ailments, such as a cold or sore throat, are very popular throughout the Caribbean. Lemongrass grows abundantly across the region and is often used in these germ-fighting recipes.

1 bunch (about 2 oz [55 g]) freshly picked lemongrass

½ cup (100 g) sugar

½ cup (120 ml) honey

Evaporated milk (optional)

Boil 2 quarts (1.9 L) of water and the lemongrass together in a pot over high heat for 20 minutes. Remove the lemongrass and pour the hot liquid into a heatproof glass or stainless-steel container. Add the sugar and honey. Serve hot. Some Virgin Islanders like to add evaporated milk. This drink can also be served iced.

BREAKFAST BUSH TEA

yield: 8 servings

In the Virgin Islands, it is quite common to walk into an office building in the morning and smell the aroma of freshly brewed bush tea, the islanders' breakfast beverage of choice. Bush tea is made from a collection of local bushes and recipes vary widely from person to person, often based on what is available in one's yard. Many of these fragrant bushes are thought to have medicinal properties and the tea is often touted to have health benefits. It's often served with a heaping scoop or two—or three!—of brown sugar. This is a caffeine-free way to start your morning right!

2 oz (55 g) freshly picked lemongrass

½ cup (48 g) firmly packed fresh mint

10 fresh basil leaves

½ cup (120 ml) honey

Dark brown sugar (optional)

In a large pot, combine 2 quarts (1.9 L) of water and the herbs and bring to a boil. Boil for 20 minutes. Remove from the heat and let it cool for 5 minutes. Strain the liquid into a large pitcher and discard the herbs. Stir the honey and brown sugar, if using, into the tea. Serve hot.

HIBISCUS-ADE

yield: 8 servings

The hibiscus flower is one of the most prolific flowers in the Virgin Islands and it can be found in a wide variety of shades. There is even a Hibiscus Society dedicated to the cultivation of these beauties. They are edible, and are actually one of the favorite foods of our local iguanas.

Hibiscus flowers also make delicious drinks! My stepmother, Alicia, in addition to being a very good cook, is also one of the most resourceful women I know. She is very good at putting anything she has on hand into a tasty meal or drink. I've drunk hibiscus-ade for most of my life, but I had never seen it made before until I saw Alicia make it. I couldn't look away! It was so intriguing to see the use of flowers in a drink! I love the smell the flowers release as they cook in hot water.

27 red hibiscus blossoms (or another edible flower of choice)

1 tbsp (8 g) grated fresh ginger

Juice of 5 limes

1½ cups (300 g) sugar, or to taste

In a large pot, combine 3 quarts (2.8 L) of water and the hibiscus blossoms and ginger. Bring to a boil, boil for 3 minutes, then remove from the heat. Cover the pot and set aside to let cool for 1½ hours. Strain into a large pitcher. Add the lime juice and sugar, stir well, then serve chilled.

HIBISCUS PUNCH

yield: 9 servings

Hibiscus punch offers a twist to the classic fruit punch. The aromatic hibiscus blooms give this punch a distinctive tangy, floral flavor. This drink is sure to be light, refreshing and the ultimate thirst-quencher. If you don't have hibiscus available where you live, take a look in your own garden and see whether you have any edible flowers growing. You may be surprised at what you find!

27 red hibiscus blooms (or another edible flower of choice)

1 tbsp (8 g) grated fresh ginger

Juice of 3 limes

2 cups (475 ml) pineapple juice

2 cups (475 ml) freshly squeezed orange juice

½ cup (120 ml) grenadine

½ cup (100 g) sugar

In a large pot, combine 2 quarts (1.9 L) of water and the hibiscus blossoms and ginger and bring to a boil. Let boil for 3 minutes, remove it from the heat and cover. Let the mixture sit for 1½ hours. Once the mixture has cooled, strain the liquid into a large pitcher. Now, add the lime juice, pineapple juice, orange juice, grenadine and sugar and stir well. Serve the punch over ice.

GINGER BEER

yield: 8 servings

Although this beverage has beer in the title, it actually is more like a health tonic. The combination of ginger and honey makes a pleasant and refreshing way to combat the common cold or an upset stomach. Well, at least that's what I grew up hearing from the older folks around me.

6 (0.5-oz [15-g]) pieces fresh ginger, washed but not peeled

1 tsp (5 ml) vanilla extract

1 cup (240 ml) honey

Grate the ginger or mince it in a food processor, then transfer to a large glass container or pitcher. Add 2 quarts (1.9 L) of water, cover and let sit overnight or for at least 4 hours at room temperature. After the resting period, strain through a fine-mesh strainer or sieve into a large pitcher. Add the vanilla, followed by the honey. Stir well until the honey is dissolved. Serve chilled or over ice. Keep refrigerated.

PEANUT PUNCH

yield: 8 servings

People in the Caribbean have been drinking peanut butter long before it became a popular protein shake additive. Peanut punch is especially popular among vegans and vegetarians because it does have such a high protein content and can easily be made dairy-free by substituting a soy- or nut-based milk. When I drink peanut punch, it's more of a snack than a drink!

1 cup (260 g) peanut butter

2 fresh or frozen bananas

4 cups (946 ml) milk or dairy-free alternative

2 tbsp (30 ml) honey

1 tsp (2 g) ground cinnamon

⅓ cup (27 g) rolled oats

Sugar (optional)

Place all the ingredients in a blender and blend on high speed until thoroughly mixed, about 2 minutes. Add sugar, if desired. Serve chilled.

SOURSOP JUICE

yield: 6 servings

Soursop is famed with island mothers for being sleep-inducing. In fact, in a moment of desperation when our son wasn't sleeping well, my wife put soursop leaves under his crib sheet. It is popular for Caribbean parents to make soursop tea or "specials" to try to encourage little ones to take a rest. My father-in-law, Maurice, is famous among his grandkids for always having "specials" as an after-dinner treat. Whenever he or his sister Luana get their hands on fresh soursop, it is promptly turned into this drink and then frozen to await the next time this large family all gets together. For me, this is one of the highlights of Wheatley family gatherings. If you haven't ever had soursop, you are in for a delightful treat. Soursop juice is so creamy and smooth and in the world of home remedies, its health benefits are famous!

1 large, ripe fresh soursop fruit
1 tsp (5 ml) almond extract
1 cup (235 ml) evaporated milk
1 cup (200 g) sugar

To begin, bring 4 cups (946 ml) of water to boil in a large pot. While the water is boiling, peel and core the fresh soursop. Place the soursop in the boiling water, then immediately remove the pot from the heat. Let the mixture sit for 1 hour. Next, set a large fine-mesh sieve over a large bowl and pour the mixture through the sieve. Using a spoon, apply pressure to the pulp in the sieve to extract any excess liquid. Now, add the almond extract, evaporated milk and sugar and stir well. Serve the juice over ice.

ANNA'S CHRISTMAS "SPIRITED" COQUITO

Yield: 16 servings

I love celebrating holidays in the Caribbean. Family from far and wide travel back to the islands to celebrate. This means there are plenty of parties to attend with food and beverages for days on end. On Christmas Day, I typically make the rounds between at least five or six different homes. It gets kind of crazy, but I wouldn't have it any other way!

Coquito is a Puerto Rican drink that most Virgin Islanders make around Christmastime. With their close proximity, the Virgin Islands and Puerto Rico have a history of cultural integration. This recipe comes from an adaptation of one that my sister-in-law makes. It takes several years and numerous batches to perfect the right balance of flavor and booziness!

2 (12-oz [355 ml]) cans cream of coconut

1 (12-oz [355-ml]) can evaporated milk

2 (12-oz [355-ml]) cans coconut milk

1 (12-oz [355-ml]) can sweetened condensed milk

2 tbsp (30 ml) vanilla extract

1 tsp (2 g) ground cinnamon

1 tsp (2 g) ground nutmeg

12 oz (355 ml) high-proof coconut-flavored rum (optional, but highly recommended!)

In a large blender, combine all the ingredients. Blend very well until the mixture is a homogenous creamy liquid. Place in a glass container and refrigerate. Serve cold.

Acknowledgments

Publishing my first cookbook is such an exciting project, one that would not have been possible without some very special people.

Mom, thank you for your awakening my love of cooking from an early age and helping me learn traditional Caribbean recipes.

To my wife, thank you for your endless support as I chase all my crazy dreams.

To my #2, Rebekah, thanks for always being a willing taste tester and my personal food critic.

Alicia, thanks for lending your ear when I needed to consult.

Dad, thanks for always pushing me to be great.

To my "catering mom" Shelly, thanks for giving me the opportunity to work for you and develop my skills.

To my in-laws, Dawn, Maurice, Anna and Luana, thanks for collaborating with me.

To my teammates, All In Sports Entertainment, your work on my behalf has taken me to new heights. Thank you for believing in me.

To Matt and Melee Media, thanks for being on this journey with me from the very inception of this idea and for sharing your knowledge.

To my friends Zach, Melinda and Kareem, thanks for encouraging me and keeping me on task, especially in the Irma/Maria aftermath.

To the My Brother's Workshop team, Mark, Jenny, Scott, Jessica, Danielle and our trainees, thanks for inspiring me, believing in me and being my taste testers!

My Aunty Anette for sharing her two cents on the proper way to curry.

My Marriott Frenchmans Reef family/Sunset Grill family, Vicky, Laban, Nazo, Cherill and the crew for starting me off on my culinary journey with my first real cooking position.

To Jennifer Blume, thank you for encouraging my cookbook dream. You are a uniquely talented photographer whose images brought my recipes to life.

Katie, Chris, Beverly, Sara, Peter and Blake, thank you for your words on my behalf. I'm humbled by your support.

To the Page Street Publishing team, especially Marissa and Meg, there would be no cookbook without you. Thank you for believing in me and giving me this opportunity. Thank you for your patience and dedication. The finished product surpasses my wildest dreams.

To my Florida Culinary Institute family, chefs and peers, thank you for helping me develop into the chef I am today.

There are countless others who have shaped me in this journey and I am extremely grateful to have the support of amazing family, friends, chefs and fellow athletes.

About the Author

Julius Jackson is a professional chef, professional boxer and 2008 Olympian who was born and raised in the US Virgin Islands. When he's not in the gym training for a fight, Julius's full-time job is as manager and head chef of My Brother's Workshop Bakery and Café, a life-skills training program for at-risk youth. Julius is also partner in a private catering company, USVI Catering, and creator of "The Chef's Cooking Lab" culinary experience. Julius has made appearances on Showtime, Food Network, the Cooking Channel and Telemundo. Julius resides in St. Thomas, US Virgin Islands, with his wife, Nicole, and son, Dominic.

Index